TRIBUNALS, COURTS AND ENFORC
2007

EXPLANATORY NOTES

INTRODUCTION

1. These explanatory notes relate to the Tribunals, Courts and Enforcement Act 2007 which received Royal Assent on 19th July 2007. They have been prepared by the Ministry of Justice in order to assist the reader of the Act. The explanatory notes have not been endorsed by Parliament.

2. The notes need to be read in conjunction with the Act. They are not, and are not meant to be, a comprehensive description of the Act. So where a section or part of a section does not seem to require any explanation or comment, none is given. Where a section makes a change to the system currently in place, an overview is given of that system followed by an explanation of the change that the Act makes.

OVERVIEW

3. The Tribunals, Courts and Enforcement Act implements the main recommendations contained in the following reports and papers:

    *   the White Paper, Transforming Public Services: Complaints, Redress and Tribunals,[1] published in July 2004 ("Transforming Public Services");

    *   the consultation paper Increasing Diversity in the Judiciary, published in October 2004;

    *   the Law Commission Report, Landlord and Tenant – Distress for Rent,[2] published in February 1991 ("the Law Commission's Report");

    *   a Report to the Lord Chancellor, Independent Review of Bailiff Law, by Professor J. Beatson QC published in July 2000;

    *   a White Paper, Effective Enforcement, published in March 2003 ("*Effective Enforcement*");

    *   a consultation paper, A Choice of Paths: better options to manage over-indebtedness and multiple debt, published on 20 July 2004 ("the Choice of Paths Consultation");

    *   a consultation paper, Relief for the Indebted, an alternative to bankruptcy, published in March 2005; and

    *   a consultation on providing immunity from seizure for international works of art on loan in the UK (March 2006).

4. The explanatory notes are divided into parts reflecting the structure of the Act. For each part, there is a summary of the provisions and commentary on the background to the proposals. Commentary on particular sections in each part is set out

---

[1] Command paper 6243
[2] February 1991, Report No. 194

in numerical order, with the commentary on the various Schedules included with the section to which they relate.

5.   The Act is divided into 8 Parts:

Part 1: Tribunals and Inquiries

Part 1 creates a new, simplified statutory framework for tribunals which provides coherence and will enable future reform. It brings the tribunal judiciary together under a Senior President. It also replaces the Council on Tribunals, the supervisory body for tribunals, with the Administrative Justice and Tribunals Council, which has been given a broader remit.

Part 2: Judicial Appointments

Part 2 provides for revised minimum eligibility requirements for appointment to judicial office, including provision to enable eligibility to be extended, by order, beyond barristers and solicitors to the holders of other relevant qualifications, such as legal executives. It also contains some other amendments relating to the selection procedure for certain judicial appointments, and the appointment of the Chairman of the Law Commission.

Part 3: Enforcement by Taking Control of Goods

Part 3 unifies the existing law relating to enforcement by seizure and sale of goods for most purposes. It also replaces the current law of rent distress with a modified regime for recovering rent arrears in the commercial property sector.

Part 4: Enforcement of Judgments and Orders

Part 4 contains measures to help creditors with claims in the civil court to enforce their judgments, including a new court-based mechanism to help the court gain access to information about the judgment debtor, on behalf of the creditor.

Part 5: Debt Management and Relief

Part 5 makes changes to two statutory debt-management schemes, administration orders and enforcement restriction orders. Part 5 also contains measures which provide debtors who are unable to pay their debts with relief from enforcement and discharge from their debts. In addition, Part 5 contains non-court based measures to help over-indebted persons and those with multiple debt situations manage their indebtedness.

Part 6: Protection of cultural objects on loan

Part 6 provides immunity from seizure to objects which have been lent to this country from overseas to be included in a temporary exhibition at a museum or gallery.

Part 7: Miscellaneous

Part 7 makes changes to the ability of High Court enforcement officers and the obligation on High Sheriffs to execute writs of possession issued to enforce compulsory purchase orders. Part 7 also amends section 31 of the Supreme Court Act 1981 ("SCA 1981") enabling the High Court to substitute its decision for that of a court or tribunal in certain circumstances. Part 7 additionally provides for enforcement of ACAS-supervised settlements of employment disputes. It also provides for appeals to go to the courts instead of to the tribunal set up by section 28 of the Registered Designs Act 1949.

Part 8: General

Part 8 contains technical provisions including those about implementation.

PART 1: TRIBUNALS AND INQUIRIES

SUMMARY

6.　　The policy intention underlying Part 1 of the Act is to create a new, simplified statutory framework for tribunals, bringing existing tribunal jurisdictions together and providing a structure for new jurisdictions and new appeal rights.

7.　　The Act provides a new unified structure by creating two new tribunals, the First-tier Tribunal and the Upper Tribunal. It gives the Lord Chancellor power to transfer the jurisdiction of existing tribunals to the two new tribunals. Further, the Lord Chancellor is empowered to transfer to himself certain statutory powers and duties in relation to the administration of tribunals. The Act places the Lord Chancellor under a general duty to provide administrative support to the new tribunals, and also to the employment tribunals, Employment Appeal Tribunal and Asylum and Immigration Tribunal (AIT).

8.　　The Act also creates a new judicial office, the Senior President of Tribunals, to oversee tribunal judiciary. The Senior President will be the judicial leader of the tribunals system. The Senior President of Tribunals holds a distinct statutory office and in carrying out the functions of that office is not subject to the direction of any other judicial office holder. The Act provides for the membership of the tribunals, rights of appeal from the tribunals and the making of new Tribunal Procedure Rules. The Act also gives the Upper Tribunal the power to exercise a judicial review jurisdiction in certain circumstances. Further, the Act also replaces the Council on Tribunals with the Administrative Justice and Tribunals Council, which will have a broader remit over the whole of the administrative justice system.

BACKGROUND

9.　　Tribunals constitute a substantial part of the justice system. They deal with a wide range of disputes including those between the individual and the state (such as benefits, tax and immigration) and between private individuals (such as employment disputes).

10.　　Until now, most tribunals have been created by individual pieces of primary legislation, without any overarching framework. Many have been administered by the government departments responsible for the policy area in which that tribunal has jurisdiction. Those departments are sometimes responsible for the decisions which are appealable to the tribunal.

11.　　In the report of his Review of Tribunals, *Tribunals for Users – One System, One Service*, published in August 2001, Sir Andrew Leggatt recommended extensive reform to the tribunals system. He recommended that tribunals should be brought together in a single system and that they should become separate from their current sponsoring departments. He recommended that such a system be administered instead by a single Tribunals Service, in what was then the Lord Chancellor's Department.

12.　　The Government agreed and published its response to the report in the White Paper *Transforming Public Services: Complaints, Redress and Tribunals* in July 2004.

The new tribunals

13.   The Government's response to Sir Andrew Leggatt's recommended single tribunal system is to create two new, generic tribunals, the First-tier Tribunal and the Upper Tribunal, into which existing tribunal jurisdictions can be transferred. The Upper Tribunal is primarily, but not exclusively, an appellate tribunal from the First-tier Tribunal.

14.   The Act also provides for the establishment of "chambers" within the two tribunals so that the many jurisdictions that will be transferred into the tribunals can be grouped together appropriately. Each chamber will be headed by a Chamber President and the tribunals' judiciary will be headed by a Senior President of Tribunals.

Membership, deployment and composition

15.   A distinctive feature of tribunals in their current form is their membership. Some tribunals consist of a lawyer sitting alone. Others comprise a lawyer sitting with one or more members who may be experts in their field (such as doctors or accountants) who have experience relevant to the work of the tribunal, or have no relevant experience but have generic skills. A few tribunals have no legal members at all.

16.   At present, there is no coherent system in place for deploying tribunal members. While some sit in more than one jurisdiction, this will be as a result of the member having gone through the whole appointments process for each additional jurisdiction.

17.   The Act creates new offices for the First-tier and Upper Tribunal. It creates new titles (giving the legal members the title of judges) and a new system of deployment. Judges of the First-tier Tribunal or Upper Tribunal will be assigned to one or more of the chambers of that tribunal, having regard to their knowledge and experience. The fact that a member may be allocated to more than one chamber allows members to be deployed across the jurisdictions within the tribunal. It is expected that the current members of transferred tribunals, apart from the General Commissioners, will become members of the new tribunals.

Reviews and appeals and the judicial review jurisdiction of the tribunals

18.   Currently there is no single mechanism for appealing against a tribunal decision. Appeal rights differ from tribunal to tribunal. In some cases there is a right of appeal to another tribunal. In other cases there is a right of appeal to the High Court. In some cases there is no right of appeal at all. The Act provides a unified appeal structure. Under the Act, in most cases, a decision of the First-tier Tribunal may be appealed to the Upper Tribunal and a decision of the Upper Tribunal may be appealed to a court. The grounds of appeal must relate to a point of law. The rights to appeal may only be exercised with permission from the tribunal being appealed from or the tribunal or court, as the case may be, being appealed to.

19.   It will also be possible for the Upper Tribunal to deal with some judicial review cases which would otherwise have to be dealt with by the High Court or Court of Session. The Upper Tribunal has this jurisdiction only where a case falls within a class specified in a direction given by the Lord Chief Justice or in certain other cases transferred by the High Court or Court of Session, but it will not be possible for cases

to be transferred to the Upper Tribunal if they involve immigration or nationality matters.

20.   Instead of tribunal rules being made by the Lord Chancellor and other government Ministers under a multiplicity of different rule-making powers, a new Tribunal Procedure Committee will be responsible for tribunal rules. This committee has been modelled on existing rule committees which make rules of court.

Transfer of tribunal functions

21.   It is intended that the new tribunals will exercise the jurisdictions currently exercised by the tribunals listed in Parts 1 to 4 of Schedule 6, which constitute most of the tribunal jurisdictions administered by central government. The Government's policy is that in the future, when a new tribunal jurisdiction is required to deal with a right of review or appeal, that right of appeal or review will be to these new tribunals.

22.   Some tribunals have been excluded from the new structures because of their specialist nature. Tribunals run by local government have for now been excluded, as their funding and sponsorship arrangements are sufficiently different to merit a separate review.

23.   There are also tribunals that will share a common administration, and the leadership of the Senior President of Tribunals, but whose jurisdictions will not be transferred to the new tribunals. They are the AIT, the employment tribunals and the Employment Appeal Tribunal. The AIT has a unique single-tier structure (as prescribed by the Nationality, Immigration and Asylum Act 2002, as amended by the Asylum and Immigration (Treatment of Claimants etc) Act 2004) which would not fit into the new structure established by the Act. The employment tribunals and the Employment Appeal Tribunal are excluded because of the nature of the cases that come before them, which involve one party against another, unlike most other tribunals which hear appeals from citizens against decisions of the State.

Administrative Support

24.   In *Transforming Public Services*, the Government set out its plans to create a single Tribunals Service to provide common administrative support to the main central government tribunals. The new Service, an executive agency of what was the Department for Constitutional Affairs (DCA) and is now the Ministry of Justice (MoJ), was launched in April 2006. It provides support to a range of tribunals, including the Asylum and Immigration Tribunal, the Social Security and Child Support Tribunals, the employment tribunals and the Employment Appeal Tribunal, and the Mental Health Review Tribunals in England. Most tribunals which are the responsibility of central government are now administered by the Tribunals Service, or will join the Service over the next few years.

25.   The Tribunals Service was created by machinery of government changes. Legislation was not required. The Act does not, therefore, set out a blueprint for the new agency. The Act does, however, give the Lord Chancellor the power to transfer to himself certain statutory powers and duties that primarily relate to the provision of administrative support for tribunals. It entrenches these powers and duties with the office of the Lord Chancellor so that they can be transferred to another minister only by primary legislation.

26.   In developing these proposals, the intention has been to follow the principles underlying the evolving constitutional settlement between the executive and the judiciary set out in the concordat agreed between the Lord Chancellor and the Lord Chief Justice for England and Wales in January 2004, and the Constitutional Reform Act 2005 ("CRA 2005").

Oversight of Tribunals and Inquiries

27.   The Council on Tribunals ("the Council") operates under the Tribunals and Inquiries Act 1992 ("the 1992 Act"). Its statutory purpose is to keep under review and report on the constitution and working of tribunals under its supervision. The Council has to consider and report on particular matters that may be referred to it under the 1992 Act with respect to tribunals and, where necessary, to consider and report on the administrative procedures of statutory inquiries. The Council is also under a statutory duty to make an annual report about its work, which is to be laid before Parliament. The Council seeks to ensure that tribunals and inquiries meet the needs of users through the provision of an open, fair, impartial, efficient, timely and accessible service.

28.   Sir Andrew Leggatt recommended that the Council on Tribunals should play a central role in the new tribunals system (recommendations 168-182). *Transforming Public Services* built on these recommendations in the wider context of the Government's proposals for reforming the Administrative Justice System. Chapter 11 of the White Paper proposed that with the creation of the Tribunals Service in April 2006 it was also necessary for the Council to change. It proposed that the Council should take on a wider remit to become an Administrative Justice and Tribunals Council and in particular to focus on the needs of the public and users.

Administrative Justice and Tribunals Council

29.   Under this Act, the Administrative Justice and Tribunals Council ("the AJTC") will adopt a role in relation to the supervision of tribunals similar to that currently exercised by the Council on Tribunals. But in addition to taking on the Council on Tribunals' current remit, the AJTC will be charged with keeping the administrative justice system as a whole under review. It is tasked with considering how to make the system more accessible, fair and efficient, and advising the Lord Chancellor, the Scottish Ministers, Welsh Ministers and the Senior President accordingly.

30.   The AJTC's wider administrative justice role will be concerned with ensuring that the relationships between the courts, tribunals, ombudsmen and alternative dispute resolution routes satisfactorily reflect the needs of users.

31.   The AJTC will be of a comparable size to the present Council on Tribunals, with between 10 and 15 members appointed by the Lord Chancellor, and by Ministers from the devolved administrations. One of those appointed members will be nominated by the Lord Chancellor, after consultation with the Scottish and Welsh Ministers, to chair the AJTC. Whereas the Council has just a Scottish Committee, the AJTC will have Scottish and Welsh Committees.

Enforcement

32.   Tribunals have no enforcement powers of their own. If a monetary award is not paid then, in England and Wales, the claimant must register it in the county court

and use the enforcement methods available there (for example see section 15 of the Employment Tribunals Act 1996). *Transforming Public Services* undertook to simplify the system so that an award of compensation, whether ordered by the tribunal or agreed between the parties (under compromises involving the Advisory, Conciliation and Arbitration Service (ACAS)), can be enforced with the minimum of bureaucracy as if it were an order of the civil courts.

33. The Act will remove the need for registration of unpaid awards in the county court or the High Court and provide that they can be enforced as if they bear the right to a warrant of execution. Claimants will be able to go directly to the county court or High Court for enforcement.

34. Essentially, the legislative changes will (a) allow claimants to proceed immediately to enforcement (levelling the playing field between tribunal users and other civil claimants), and (b) ensure that those owed money as a result of a tribunal hearing can benefit from improvements to the wider civil enforcement system.

35. The procedure for enforcing tribunal awards in England and Wales (and Northern Ireland), and ACAS brokered agreements (see section 142), will become similar to the Scottish process, in that the award will be treated as enforceable without any intermediate steps being necessary. Part 1 of the Act does not alter the methods of enforcement either in Scotland or in England and Wales (or Northern Ireland), but allows tribunals to benefit from them.

36. In addition, the Act provides for unpaid awards to be entered on the Register of Judgments, Orders and Fines, see paragraph 55 of Schedule 8, (which may be searched by banks, building societies, and credit companies when considering applications for credit). The Act also makes it easier for the courts to obtain information about the debtor, as claimants will be able to make information requests under the provisions contained in Part 4 of the Act, which will help them to identify what kind of court action it would be appropriate to take to recover the debt.

COMMENTARY ON SECTIONS: PART 1

Section 1: Independence of tribunal judiciary

37. Section 1 ensures that the duty imposed on the Lord Chancellor and other Ministers of the Crown under the Constitutional Reform Act 2005 (the CRA 2005), to uphold the continued independence of the judiciary, extends to all of the tribunal judges where a tribunal is administered by the Lord Chancellor. To do this, the definition of "the judiciary" in section 3 of the CRA 2005 is amended to make it clear that, so far as they are not already included within that definition, all office-holders listed in Schedule 14 to that Act, and certain additional tribunal office-holders are within that definition.

Section 2 and Schedule 1: Senior President of Tribunals

Section 2

38. Section 2 creates a new statutory judicial post - that of Senior President of Tribunals. The post is intended to provide unified leadership to the tribunals judiciary. The creation of the post was recommended by Sir Andrew Leggatt in his review.

39.   Subsection (1) stipulates that the Senior President is to be appointed by HM the Queen on the recommendation of the Lord Chancellor.

40.   The Act creates a number of specific powers and duties for the Senior President, including:

- his concurrence in relation to the chambers structure for the First-tier Tribunal and the Upper Tribunal (and any change in it) (section 7(1));

- that he may, with the concurrence of the Lord Chancellor, make provision for the allocation of functions between chambers (section 7(9));

- his duty to report to the Lord Chancellor on matters which the Senior President wishes to bring to the attention of the Lord Chancellor and matters which the Lord Chancellor has asked the Senior President to cover (section 43);

- his power to make practice directions (section 23);

- the right to be consulted on the making of fees orders (section 42(5));

- his concurrence in relation to the making of orders prescribing the qualifications required for appointment of members of the First-tier Tribunal (Schedule 2, paragraph 2(2)) and the Upper Tribunal (Schedule 3, paragraph 2(2));

- the power to request a judge of the First-tier Tribunal or the Upper Tribunal to act as a judge of those tribunals (Schedule 2 paragraph 6(2); Schedule 3 paragraph 6(2));

- the duty to maintain appropriate arrangements for training, welfare and guidance of judges and other members (Schedule 2 paragraph 8; Schedule 3 paragraph 9);

- the duty to co-operate with the Lord Chief Justices of England and Wales and Northern Ireland, and the Lord President in relation to the training, welfare and guidance of the tribunals judiciary (section 47);

- the power to take oaths of allegiance and judicial oaths (or to nominate someone to do so) from judges and other members of the First-tier and Upper Tribunal (Schedule 2 paragraph 9, and Schedule 3 paragraph 10) and Chamber Presidents, Deputy Chamber Presidents and Acting Chamber presidents (Schedule 4, paragraph 8). Employment tribunal presidents and panel members, and their counterparts in the EAT are covered in Schedule 8 (paragraphs 40 and 44), as are Criminal Injuries Compensation Appeals Panel (CICAP) adjudicators (at paragraph 34);

- the right to be consulted before the Lord Chancellor appoints a Chamber President from among the ranks of the judiciary (Schedule 4, paragraph 2(1));

- the power to assign judges and other members to chambers (Schedule 4, paragraph 9);

- being or nominating a member of the Tribunal Procedure Committee (it is expected that the Senior President or his nominee will chair the Committee) (Schedule 5 paragraph 20);

- the power to request the appointment of additional members of the Tribunal Procedure Committee (Schedule 5 paragraph 24).

41.　　Subsection (3) sets out principles that the Senior President has to have regard to when exercising the powers of the office. These criteria are based on the long-standing principles underlying the jurisdiction of tribunals, as originally articulated by the Report of the Committee on Administrative Tribunals and Inquiries in 1957 (the Franks Report).

Schedule 1

42.　　Schedule 1 sets out the process for appointing a Senior President and the terms of his office. This is a judicial appointment. The appointment is made by Her Majesty the Queen (section 2(1)), in line with the practice for senior judicial appointments generally. Her Majesty acts on the recommendation of the Lord Chancellor.

43.　　Paragraph 1 provides that if there is a vacancy, the Lord Chancellor must recommend a person for appointment to the office unless the Lord Chief Justice agrees that it may remain unfilled.

44.　　Paragraph 2 provides that there are two alternative routes for the Lord Chancellor to make a recommendation in relation to the appointment of the Senior President. The first is where the Lord Chancellor, the Lord Chief Justice of England and Wales, the Lord President of the Court of Session and the Lord Chief Justice of Northern Ireland agree on the nomination of a Lord or Lady Justice of Appeal or a member of the Inner House of the Court of Session as a suitable candidate for appointment. In such circumstances the Lord Chancellor must recommend the person for appointment unless that person refuses the recommendation or does not agree to the recommendation within a specified time or is otherwise not available to be recommended within a certain time. The second route applies when there is no such agreement. In those circumstances the Lord Chancellor must ask the Judicial Appointments Commission to select someone for recommendation for appointment.

45.　　Paragraphs 3 to 5 set out the process for selection by the Judicial Appointments Commission. It follows as closely as is appropriate the criteria and process for appointment of Heads of Division of the High Court under sections 67 to 75 of the CRA 2005.

46.　　Paragraph 3 provides that the eligibility requirement for the Senior President is the same as the eligibility requirement for a Lord or Lady Justice of Appeal, once amended by paragraph 13(2) of Schedule 10 to the Act.

47.　　Paragraph 4 inserts seven new sections into the CRA 2005. These sections create a process for the selection of the Senior President by the Judicial Appointments Commission which is the same as the process for appointment of a Head of Division of the High Court, except that the Lord President of the Court of Session and the Lord Chief Justice of Northern Ireland are consulted, because the Senior President has United Kingdom-wide responsibilities. The selection panel for the appointment of the Senior President consists of the Lord Chief Justice, or his nominee, a person designated by the Lord Chief Justice, the Chairman of the Commission or his nominee and a lay member of the Commission designated by the third member. The person designated by the Lord Chief Justice is intended to be a present or former office holder in tribunals to bring to the selection panel direct knowledge or experience of the distinctive nature of tribunals in the justice system.

48.   Paragraphs 6 to 10 set out the terms of office for the Senior President. The Senior President may be appointed either for a fixed term or for an indefinite period subject only to the retirement provisions of the Judicial Pensions and Retirement Act 1993. The Senior President may only be removed from office by Her Majesty on an address presented to Her by both Houses of Parliament.

49.   The Senior President may resign at any time. If the Lord Chancellor, the Lord Chief Justice of England and Wales, the Lord President of the Court of Session and the Lord Chief Justice of Northern Ireland agree that the holder of the office is disabled by permanent infirmity and is incapacitated from resigning, the Lord Chancellor may instead declare the holder to have vacated the office.

50.   Paragraph 11 provides that on appointment, the Senior President must take the oath of allegiance and the judicial oath (as set out in the Promissory Oaths Act 1868), in the presence of the Lord Chief Justice of England and Wales or another holder of high judicial office nominated by the Lord Chief Justice.

51.   Paragraphs 12 to 14 describe the powers and responsibilities of the Senior President in relation to making representations to Parliament and Ministers about matters he considers to be of importance to tribunal judiciary and other members and matters relating to the administration of justice by tribunals. Paragraph 14 makes it clear that responsibility for representing the views of tribunal judiciary and other members to Parliament, and to the Lord Chancellor and Ministers of the Crown generally, rests with the Senior President of Tribunals.

Section 3: The First-tier Tribunal and the Upper Tribunal

52.   Section 3 provides for the creation of a First-tier Tribunal and an Upper Tribunal, each consisting of judges (i.e. legally qualified members) and other members, and presided over by the Senior President of Tribunals. It is intended that the Upper Tribunal will primarily, but not exclusively, be an appellate tribunal from the First-tier Tribunal. The new tribunals are intended to be adaptable institutions, able to take on any existing or new tribunal jurisdictions. So in the future, when Parliament decides to create a new appeal right or jurisdiction, it will not have to create a new tribunal to administer it. The Upper Tribunal is a superior court of record, like the High Court and the Employment Appeal Tribunal.

Section 4 and Schedule 2: Judges and other members of the First-tier Tribunal

53.   Section 4 and Schedule 2 set out provisions relating to judges and other members of the First-tier Tribunal.

Section 4

54.   Section 4 lists those persons who are to be the judges and other members of the First-tier Tribunal.

55.   At present most tribunals include legally qualified members and members without a legal qualification. The qualification requirements which apply to the lawyers, who often chair the tribunal hearing a case, are varied. The range of non-legal members is very wide and includes members such as medical practitioners, accountants, people with experience of disability issues, people with experience of the armed services and so-called "lay" members. This structure will continue in the new tribunals, with the legally qualified members of the First-tier Tribunal being called judges of the First-tier Tribunal.

56.   Judges and other members of the new tribunals will either be transferred in from existing tribunals, be appointed as such ("appointed judges/members"), or hold their office in the First-tier Tribunal by virtue of another office which they hold. So, for example, a circuit judge will automatically be a member of each of the First-tier Tribunal or the Upper Tribunal (by virtue of sections 4(1)(c), 5(1)(g) and 6). This will enable judges who have the appropriate expertise and experience, from holding judicial office in courts or other tribunals, to be brought into the new tribunals to help to deal with the tribunals' work. Similarly, some members of other tribunals without legal qualifications will automatically be members of the new tribunals. The same principle will apply within the structure of the new tribunals, so that, for example, a judge of the Upper Tribunal will automatically be a judge of the First-tier Tribunal (section 4(1)(c)).

Schedule 2

57.   Paragraph 1(2) provides that a person is eligible for appointment as a judge of the First-tier Tribunal if he has a legal qualification and 5 years' legal experience since qualifying.

58.   But in addition, persons may be appointed if, in the Lord Chancellor's opinion, they have legal experience which would make them as suitable for appointment as if they had the relevant legal qualifications. This provision, which is based on current eligibility requirements in relation to the Asylum and Immigration Tribunal and the Mental Health Review Tribunal, recognises that in the specialised fields in which tribunals operate, the necessary skills and knowledge may have been acquired by someone who does not have a professional qualification in the United Kingdom, such as a legal academic or someone qualified in a European or Commonwealth jurisdiction.

59.   Paragraph 1(1) and 2(1) state that appointed judges and members of the First-tier Tribunal are appointed by the Lord Chancellor. Except where a member of an existing tribunal is transferred into the new tribunals under section 31(2), appointment takes place after selection by the Judicial Appointments Commission.

60.   Paragraph 3 provides that appointed and transferred-in judges and other members of the First-tier Tribunal are protected by a prohibition on removal without the concurrence of the Lord Chief Justice of England and Wales, or if appropriate, the Lord President of the Court of Session or Lord Chief Justice of Northern Ireland.

61.   Paragraph 4 ensures that appointed and transferred-in judges and other members of the First-tier Tribunal who are appointed on a salaried as opposed to a fee paid basis have the further protection of a provision that they may be only removed by the Lord Chancellor on the ground of inability or misbehaviour.

62.   Both paragraphs 3 and 4 are intended to safeguard the independence of the tribunals.

63.   Paragraphs 6 and 7 provide for ex-officio judges and members of the First-tier Tribunal. As mentioned above, the judges and members of the First-tier Tribunal will be made up partly of ex officio judges and members, i.e. those who hold office in the new tribunals by virtue of other offices they hold in the courts or tribunals. The deployment of those ex officio judges and members is to be under the control of the Senior President of Tribunals, in conjunction, in the case of judges from the courts, with the Lord Chief Justice of England and Wales, the Lord President of the Court of

Session or the Lord Chief Justice of Northern Ireland. Part 2 of Schedule 4 deals with the assignment of these judges and members to chambers.

64.   Paragraph 8 ensures that the Senior President of Tribunals has responsibility for maintaining arrangements for the training, welfare and guidance of judges and other members of the First-tier Tribunal.

65.   Paragraph 9 makes provision for judges and members of the First-tier Tribunal to take the oath of allegiance and the judicial oath before the Senior President of Tribunals, or before an eligible person nominated by the Senior President. The requirement under paragraph 9 does not apply, however, in the case of transferred-in judges or transferred-in other members who have already taken the required oaths after accepting another office. Judges and members who carry out functions mainly or wholly in Northern Ireland may be required to take instead the oath, or the affirmation and declaration, set out in section 19 of the Justice (Northern Ireland) Act 2002.

Section 5 and Schedule 3: Judges and other members of the Upper Tribunal

66.   Section 5 and Schedule 3 set out provisions relating to the membership of the Upper Tribunal.

Section 5

67.   Section 5 lists those persons who are to be the judges and other members of the Upper Tribunal. Judges and members of an existing tribunal transferred into the Upper Tribunal under section 31(2) will automatically become judges and members of the Upper Tribunal (and of the First-Tier Tribunal) without further appointment.

Schedule 3

68.   Paragraph 1(2) provides that a person is eligible for appointment as a judge of the Upper Tribunal if he has 7 years of post-qualification experience (this is a standard qualification for judicial office). In addition, a person may be appointed to the Upper Tribunal if, in the Lord Chancellor's opinion, he has gained experience in law which makes him as suitable for appointment as if he satisfied the 7-year qualification. Appointed judges of the Upper Tribunal are appointed by the Queen, on the recommendation of the Lord Chancellor. Appointment takes place after selection by the Judicial Appointments Commission.

69.   Paragraph 3 ensures that appointed and transferred-in judges and other members of the Upper Tribunal are protected by a prohibition on removal unless there is first concurrence of the Lord Chief Justice of England and Wales, or if appropriate, the Lord President of the Court of Session or Lord Chief Justice of Northern Ireland.

70.   Paragraph 4 provides that appointed and transferred-in judges and other members of the Upper Tribunal appointed on a salaried basis have the further protection that they may be removed only by the Lord Chancellor on the ground of inability or misbehaviour.

71.   Both paragraphs 3 and 4 ensure that the independence of the tribunals is safeguarded.

72.   Paragraph 6 allows for judges of the Upper Tribunal to be made up partly of judges by request of the Senior President of Tribunals. Their deployment is to be under the control of the Senior President of Tribunals in conjunction with the Lord

Chief Justice of England and Wales, or if appropriate, the Lord President of the Court of Session or the Lord Chief Justice of Northern Ireland.

73.   Paragraph 7 provides the Lord Chancellor with the power to appoint deputy judges of the Upper Tribunal. A person must have the same legal qualifications for appointment as a deputy judge as for appointment as a judge of the Upper Tribunal. The provision will enable the appointment to the Upper Tribunal of members with particular areas of expertise.

74.   Paragraph 9 ensures that the Senior President of Tribunals has responsibility for maintaining arrangements for the training, welfare and guidance of judges and other members of the Upper Tribunal.

75.   Paragraph 10 makes provision for judges and members of the Upper Tribunal to take the oath of allegiance and the judicial oath before the Senior President of Tribunals, or before an eligible person nominated by the Senior President. The requirement under paragraph 10 does not apply, however, in the case of transferred-in judges or transferred-in other members who have already taken the required oaths after accepting another office. Judges and members who carry out functions mainly or wholly in Northern Ireland may be required to take instead the oath, or the affirmation and declaration, set out in section 19 of the Justice (Northern Ireland) Act 2002.

Section 6: Certain Judges who are also judges of First-tier Tribunal and Upper Tribunal

76.   Section 6 lists which judges are to be considered as members of both the First-tier Tribunal and the Upper Tribunal within England, Wales, Scotland and Northern Ireland by virtue of their judicial office in the courts. Temporary office holders or deputies are not included within the list.

Section 7: Chambers: Jurisdiction and Presidents and Schedule 4: Chambers and Chamber Presidents: further provision

77.   Section 7 and Schedule 4 make provision for the organisation of the First-tier and Upper Tribunal into Chambers.

Section 7

78.   Currently, many separate tribunals deal with different jurisdictions. When these tribunals are replaced by just two tribunals, it will be necessary for the jurisdictions in the new tribunals to have an organisational structure. Section 7 provides for the establishment of boundaries for the jurisdictions within the First-tier and Upper Tribunal through the creation of chambers. The tribunals will bring together a wide range of specialist jurisdictions. It would dilute expertise and damage the service provided to the public if they were organised on the basis that all judges and members can deal with all kinds of case. Instead, jurisdictions will be grouped so that similar work is dealt with by judges and members with the relevant skills to deal with it. The chambers system is intended to be flexible so that changes can be made easily to those boundaries as the workload of the tribunals changes.

79.   Subsection (1) provides that the Lord Chancellor, with the concurrence of the Senior President, will have the power to make provision for the organisation of each of the First-tier and Upper Tribunal into a number of Chambers. It makes provision for the structure of the tribunals to change over time: chambers may be merged and new chambers may be created

80.   Jurisdictions within the First-tier and Upper Tribunals will be organised into chambers so that jurisdictions which are similar in nature are grouped together. The chamber structure is intended to facilitate judicial deployment (as judiciary with expertise across the chamber can be deployed on more than one type of case). The chamber structure is also intended to facilitate judicial development and the preservation of expertise where appropriate.

81.   Subsection (2) states that for each chamber within the First-tier Tribunal and Upper Tribunal there must be a person, or two persons, to preside over that chamber. A person cannot preside over more than one chamber within the First-tier Tribunal at the same time. Likewise, a person cannot preside over more than one chamber within the Upper Tribunal at the same time, although they can preside over one chamber of the First-tier Tribunal and over one chamber of the Upper Tribunal at the same time (section 7(3)).

82.   Subsection (4) confers the title Chamber President on someone appointed to preside over a chamber.

83. Subsection (9) provides for the Senior President and the Lord Chancellor, each with the concurrence of the other, to be able to vary by order the distribution of functions between the chambers in either the First-tier Tribunal or the Upper Tribunal. Chambers may be constructed on either a functional or a geographical basis, or a combination of the two.

84. It seems likely that Chambers will evolve over time, in response to:

- the transfer of functions of other tribunals to the First-tier or Upper Tribunals;

- changes in original decisions (for example as the social security benefit system evolves);

- the creation of new areas of appeal (for example as has recently occurred in connection with the regulation of licensed gambling);

or in relation to the prevalence of a particular jurisdiction at a point in time, and other business and user needs. This may involve any or all of the following:

- Establishment of new chambers;

- Addition of jurisdictions to existing chambers;

- Transfer of functions and/or jurisdictions between chambers.

Schedule 4

85.   Schedule 4 makes further provision about chambers and Chamber Presidents.

86.   Paragraphs 1 and 5 provide for the eligibility requirements to be a Chamber President or a Deputy Chamber President to be the same as those for appointment as a judge of the Upper Tribunal under Schedule 3.

87.   Paragraphs 2 and 3 deal with the appointment of Chamber Presidents. This is a judicial leadership role involving particular skills and experience and as such it is a separate appointment under the Act. A Chamber President may (although need not) be drawn from the judiciary of the High Court or the Court of Session in Scotland or Court of Appeal in Northern Ireland. Before making an appointment from amongst the judges of those courts, the Lord Chancellor must first consult the Senior President

of Tribunals. If the Lord Chancellor decides that the appointee should be from the senior judiciary, he must seek a nomination from the Lord Chief Justice of England and Wales or Northern Ireland, or the Lord President of the Court of Session. If a suitable candidate is not forthcoming, selection will be made by the JAC. The office of Chamber President will be added to Part 3 of Schedule 14 to the CRA 2005 for this purpose (Schedule 8 paragraph 66).

88.   Paragraph 4 permits a Chamber President to delegate functions of his office to any judge or other member of the First-Tier or Upper Tribunal, or to a member of staff.

89.   Paragraph 5 provides for the appointment of Deputy Chamber Presidents. Deputy Presidents are appointed by the Lord Chancellor after consultation with the Senior President of Tribunals and are intended to be available to take on functions delegated to them by the Senior President or the Chamber President. The appointment process for Deputy Chamber Presidents mirrors that for Chamber Presidents.

90.   Paragraph 6 allows for the Senior President of Tribunals to appoint Acting Chamber Presidents to cover a temporary vacancy in the office of Chamber President.

91.   Paragraph 7 places a duty on a Chamber President to make arrangements for the issuing of guidance (to for example judges, members and users) on changes to the law and practice relating to the jurisdictions assigned to his chamber.

92.   Paragraph 8 provides for persons appointed as Chamber Presidents, or Deputy or Acting Chamber Presidents, to take the oath of allegiance and the judicial oath before the Senior President of Tribunals, or before an eligible person nominated by the Senior President

93.   Paragraph 9 makes it clear that the assigning of judges and other members to chambers of the Tribunals is a function of the Senior President.

94.   Paragraphs 10 to 12 provide that Chamber Presidents and Deputy Chamber Presidents are deemed to be assigned to the chamber(s) over which they hold office. Every other judge or member who is appointed under Schedule 2 or 3, or transferred in under section 31(2), must be assigned to at least one chamber. The process of assignment is intended to be flexible, informal and transparent. It is intended to be based upon the principle of deploying judges and members who have, or are able to acquire, the necessary skills and experience to meet identified business needs of the tribunal.

95.   Paragraph 13 obliges the Senior President to publish his policy on assignments of tribunal judges and members to chambers. This is intended to ensure openness and transparency of the system of assignment. The policy must ensure that appropriate use is made of the knowledge and experience of the judges and other members of the new tribunals. The policy must also ensure that a chamber which involves the application of the law of Scotland or Northern Ireland has enough members with knowledge and experience of those jurisdictions.

96. To ensure appropriate executive accountability to Parliament for the process of assigning members, and to take into account any resource implications, the concurrence of the Lord Chancellor will be required before the policy can be adopted.

97. Paragraph 14 provides for the allocation of members to hear individual cases. This is a judicial leadership function and therefore a matter for the Senior President.

However, this is subject to the panel composition requirements set by the Lord Chancellor in an order under paragraph 15.

98. Paragraph 15 requires the Lord Chancellor to set requirements, on a jurisdiction by jurisdiction basis, for the number of judges and other members to decide particular appeals. This order is made by the Lord Chancellor to enable him to take account of resource implications, and to provide parliamentary scrutiny.

Section 8: Senior President of Tribunals: power to delegate

99. Section 8 enables the Senior President to delegate any of his functions to any judge or member of the First-tier or Upper Tribunal or any member of staff, with the exception of his function under section 7(9) of allocating tribunal functions between the chambers of the First-tier and Upper Tribunals by order made with the concurrence of the Lord Chancellor.

Sections 9 and 10: Review of decisions of First-tier and Upper Tribunals

100. Sections 9 and 10 provide powers for the First-tier and Upper Tribunals to review their own decisions without the need for a full onward appeal and, where the tribunal concludes that an error was made, to re-decide the matter. This is intended to capture decisions that are clearly wrong, so avoiding the need for an appeal. The power has been provided in the form of a discretionary power for the Tribunal so that only appropriate decisions are reviewed. This contrasts with cases where an appeal on a point of law is made, because, for instance, it is important to have an authoritative ruling.

101. Under section 9, the First-tier Tribunal may review a decision made within the tribunal, either of its own initiative or on application by any party who has a right of appeal in respect of the decision. The tribunal has the power to correct accidental errors in the decision or in a record of the decision, amend the reasons given for the decision or set aside the decision. If a decision of the First-tier Tribunal is set aside by the First-tier Tribunal, it must either re-decide the matter concerned, or refer the matter to the Upper Tribunal. If the latter option is taken, the Upper Tribunal will then be responsible for re-deciding the matter.

102. No decision of the First-tier Tribunal may be reviewed more than once, and a decision of the tribunal not to review a decision is not reviewable or appealable. Further challenge of a decision beyond the single review may only be made by appeal on a point of law.

103. Section 10 provides corresponding review powers for the Upper Tribunal - the only difference being that if the decision is set aside by the Upper Tribunal, it must then re-decide the matter concerned (subsection (5)).

104. Sections 9(3) and 10(3) enable these wide review powers to be limited by making them subject to Tribunal Procedure Rules. They allow Rules to:

- exclude from review decisions of a description specified in the rules, whether by the tribunal of its own initiative, or on application by the parties;

- for decisions of a description specified in the rules, only allow review by the tribunal of its own initiative;

- specify in the rules the grounds on which an application for review may be brought and the grounds on which the tribunal can review of its own initiative.

These could be the same or different grounds (e.g. there may be no specified grounds for the tribunal to review of its own initiative, but specified grounds upon which a party could make an application).

105.   In summary, an exclusion or ground specified in the Rules may apply only to applications from parties or also to the tribunal acting of its own initiative (e.g. rules may state that parties in social security cases are excluded from applying for review but the tribunal may review of its own initiative in such cases).

Section 11: Right to appeal to Upper Tribunal

106.   A party to a case generally has a right of appeal on a point of law from the First-tier Tribunal to the Upper Tribunal. The right of appeal is subject to permission being given, following application by the party, by either the First-tier Tribunal or the Upper Tribunal. But there is no right of appeal against a decision which is "excluded". Excluded decisions are listed in subsection (5). The Lord Chancellor has a limited power to add to the list by order under subsection (5)(f).

107.   The basic pattern of appeal rights will for the most part remain as they are now when jurisdictions transfer to the new tribunal. Where there is currently a right of appeal, it will also exist after transfer. Where decisions currently carry no appeal rights, the transfer of the jurisdiction to the First-tier Tribunal will give rise to new onward-appeal rights unless an order excluding such rights is made under section 11(5)(f) in reliance on section 11(6)(b).

108.   In some jurisdictions it is not possible to appeal from the decision of a tribunal, even on a point of law. Equally, in some jurisdictions, tribunals hear appeals on a range of grounds which are not restricted to a point of law. Where there are currently no appeal rights in transferring jurisdictions the continuation of that exclusion will fall to be reviewed in deciding whether to exercise the power under section 11(5)(f) and (6)(b).

109.   Subsection (6) limits the Lord Chancellor's power to add to the list of excluded decisions. As a result, the power can be used for two purposes only. The first purpose is the preservation of existing appeal rights where those rights are, or include, something other than a right to appeal on a point of law. The second purpose is the preservation, in cases where there is currently no appeal right, of the existing position.

110.   Subsection (8) empowers the Lord Chancellor to specify who may or may not be treated as being a party to a case for the purposes of making an appeal from the First-tier Tribunal to the Upper Tribunal. In some cases it will be appropriate for a person who was neither the person making the original appeal to the First-tier Tribunal, nor the respondent to the original appeal, to make an onward appeal to the Upper Tribunal. At present, for instance, some rights of appeal under social security legislation to the Social Security and Child Support Commissioners are not limited to the claimant and the Secretary of State, but may include trades unions and claimants' spouses.

111.   Existing provisions in respect of who may be a party to a case for the purposes of making an appeal from the First-tier to the Upper Tribunal are expected to be preserved at the point of transfer. The power under subsection (8) may also be used in the future as new appeal rights are introduced.

112.   This power is subject to affirmative resolution procedure (see section 49).

Section 12: Proceedings on appeal to Upper Tribunal

113.   Section 12 provides for the Upper Tribunal's powers when it determines that an error has been made on a point of law by the First-tier Tribunal. The Upper Tribunal may set aside the decision of the First-tier Tribunal; if it does it must either remit the case back to the First-tier Tribunal with directions for its reconsideration, or make the decision which it considers should have been made. If it takes the latter option it can make findings of fact. If the Upper Tribunal sends the case back to the First-tier Tribunal it may direct that a different panel reconsiders the case. The Upper Tribunal may also give procedural directions in relation to the case. If the Upper Tribunal decides that the error of law does not invalidate the decision of the First-tier Tribunal it can let that decision stand.

Section 13: Right to appeal to Court of Appeal etc

114.   Section 13 provides the basis on which appeals can be made to the Court of Appeal in England and Wales or Northern Ireland or the Court of Session in Scotland. Appeals may be made on any point of law with permission either from the Upper Tribunal or the relevant appellate court (see subsection (11)). Certain decisions are excluded and the Lord Chancellor can under subsection (8)(f) add to the list, but subject to the same constraints as in section 11.

115.   Those constraints are set out in subsection (9). As a result, the power to add to the list of excluded decisions can be used for two purposes only. The first purpose is the preservation of existing appeal rights where those rights are, or include, something other than a right of appeal on a point of law. The second purpose is the preservation, in cases where there is currently no appeal right, of the existing position.

116.   Under subsection (6) the Lord Chancellor may by order restrict appeals to the Court of Appeal to cases where the court or the Upper Tribunal considers that the proposed appeal would raise some important point of principle or practice or that there is some other compelling reason for the appeal to be heard. The intention is to restrict second appeals on the same point unless there is wider public interest, i.e. where a prospective appellant has had their case considered by both the First-tier Tribunal and the Upper Tribunal. The criteria set out in this subsection are the same as the criteria applied by the Court of Appeal in considering second appeals from the High Court or county court (see the Access to Justice Act 1999, section 55(1)).

117.   The exercise of the power under the subsection is subject to the affirmative resolution procedure (see section 49). Subsection (6) does not apply to appeals to the Court of Session.

118.   Subsections (11) to (13) require the Upper Tribunal to specify the relevant appellate court (see subsection (11)). This provision is intended to deal with situations where it is not obvious which is the appropriate appellate court, e.g. where an appellant has moved from Scotland to England or vice versa, or in order that linked cases can be dealt with in the same court.

119.   Subsection (14) empowers the Lord Chancellor to specify who may or may not be treated as being a party to a case for the purposes of making an appeal from the First-tier Tribunal to the Upper Tribunal (see the note above on section 11(8)).

120.   Subsection (15) enables rules of court to specify the time within which an application for permission (or leave) may be made for a proposed appeal from the Upper Tribunal to the relevant appeal court. Any such rules for England and Wales will be made by the Civil Procedure Rules Committee.

Section 14: Proceedings on appeal to Court of Appeal etc

121.   Where the appellate court determines that the Upper Tribunal has made an error of law, it has power to set aside the decision and either send the case back to the Upper Tribunal to be redecided (or, where the decision of the Upper Tribunal was on an appeal or reference from another tribunal or some other person, to that other tribunal or person, with direction for its reconsideration), or to make the decision which it considers the Upper Tribunal (or the other tribunal or person) should have made. Under subsection (3), the appellate court may direct that the persons chosen to reconsider the case are not those who made the decision which gave rise to the appeal. It may also give procedural directions in connection with the reconsideration of the case.

"Judicial Review" Sections 15 to 21

122.   Tribunals currently have no powers of judicial review. Sections 15 to 21 create a statutory regime which enables the Upper Tribunal to exercise judicial review powers in appropriate cases. This will allow the parties to have the benefit of the specialist expertise of the Upper Tribunal in cases similar to those with which the Upper Tribunal routinely deals in the exercise of its statutory appellate jurisdiction. These provisions do not alter the inherent or statutory jurisdiction of the High Court (as amended by section 141), except as a result of the amendments made by section 19.

123.   There will be two situations in which the Upper Tribunal will be able to use these powers in cases arising under the law of England and Wales or of Northern Ireland. The first is where a direction has been made by the Lord Chief Justice or his delegate with the agreement of the Lord Chancellor, specifying a class of case to be dealt with by the Upper Tribunal rather than the High Court. The second is where the High Court orders the transfer of an individual case because it considers it just and convenient to do so in cases arising under the law of England and Wales or of Northern Ireland (but it will not be possible for cases to be transferred to the Upper Tribunal if they involve immigration or nationality matters).

Section 15: Upper Tribunal's "judicial review" jurisdiction

124.   Section 15 confers power on the Upper Tribunal to grant certain forms of relief in the same way as the High Court on an application for judicial review. This section needs to be read alongside sections 16 and 18, which set out the circumstances in which the Upper Tribunal has jurisdiction.

125.   Where it has jurisdiction, the Upper Tribunal may grant a mandatory order (an order that the respondent does something); a prohibiting order (an order that the respondent stops doing something); a quashing order (an order setting aside a decision); a declaration; or an injunction. These remedies have the same effect as if made by the High Court. In determining whether to grant a remedy, the Tribunal must have regard to the principles of judicial review that would apply in the court from which jurisdiction has been delegated. Therefore the Upper Tribunal's powers are similar to those of the High Court.

Section 16: Application for relief under section 15(1)

126.   Because the Upper Tribunal's powers are similar to those of the High Court in judicial review cases, the Upper Tribunal's powers are subject to similar conditions. Therefore it is necessary to have permission to apply to the Upper Tribunal to exercise its judicial review jurisdiction. This may not be granted if the applicant has insufficient interest in the disputed matter. The Upper Tribunal may also refuse permission, or refuse a remedy, if there has been delay in making an application.

127.   Awards made by the Upper Tribunal in exercising its judicial review jurisdiction may be enforced as if they were an award of the High Court.

Section 17: Quashing orders under section 15(1): supplementary provision

128.   Section 17 makes further provision as to the powers of the Upper Tribunal if it decides to grant a quashing order. If it quashes a decision it may also remit the matter for further consideration or substitute its own decision. The Upper Tribunal's powers are similar to the High Court's (see section 141).

Section 18: Limits of jurisdiction under section 15(1)

129.   Section 18 sets out the conditions that need to be met for the Upper Tribunal to have power to deal with an application under section 15 for relief, or an application for permission to apply for relief.

130.   Subsection (2) stipulates that four conditions must be met before the tribunal may decide the application. These are set out in subsections (4) to (8). If these conditions are not met, the tribunal must by order transfer the application to the High Court (subsection (3)).

131.   The first condition (subsection (4)) is that the applicant in question is only seeking a remedy that the Upper Tribunal is able to grant.

132.   The second condition (subsection (5)) is that the application does not call into question anything done by the Crown Court. This is because it would be anomalous to give a tribunal, a superior court of record, supervisory powers over another superior court of record.

133.   The third condition (subsection (6)) is that the application falls within a specified class of case. The class is designated by a direction made by or on behalf of the Lord Chief Justice with the concurrence of the Lord Chancellor. By virtue of subsection (7), the power to give such directions includes the power to vary or revoke directions that are made, and the power to make different provision for different circumstances.

134.   The fourth condition (subsection (8)) is that the judge presiding at the hearing of the application is either a judge listed in paragraph (a) of that subsection or a person within paragraph (b) of that subsection.

135.   Subsection (9) stipulates that where an application is transferred to the High Court under subsection (3) above, it must be treated as if it had been made to the High Court in the first place. Under subsection (10), Rules of Court may be made to enable applications, permission or leave to be treated as if they had been made by the High Court. Any such rules for England and Wales will be made by the Civil Procedure Rules Committee.

Section 19: Transfer of judicial review applications from High Court

136.   Section 19 amends the Supreme Court Act 1981 and the Judicature (Northern Ireland) Act 1978 to complement sections 15 to 18. As a result, certain applications for judicial review will have to be transferred to the Upper Tribunal where that class of case has been designated by a direction. In addition, the High Court may transfer to the Upper Tribunal individual cases that do not fall within a class specified under section 18(6). However, cases relating to immigration and nationality matters cannot be transferred in exercise of this discretionary transfer power.

Section 20: Transfer of judicial review applications from the Court of Session

137.   Section 20 makes provision for the Court of Session to transfer applications for judicial review to the Upper Tribunal. Applications cannot be transferred if they relate to immigration or nationality matters, or if they relate to devolved matters. Also, an application can only be transferred if it does not seek anything other than an exercise of the supervisory jurisdiction of the Court of Session. Subject to those three points, an application will have to be transferred if it falls within a class specified by act of sederunt made with the consent of the Lord Chancellor, and may be transferred even if it does not fall within such a class.

Section 21: Upper Tribunal's "judicial review" jurisdiction: Scotland

138.   Section 21 confirms that the Upper Tribunal will decide applications transferred to it from the Court of Session under section 20 and that the Upper Tribunal has the same powers of judicial review in such cases as the Court of Session.

Section 22 and Schedule 5: Tribunal Procedure Rules

Section 22

139.   At present, each tribunal has its own rules, and in many tribunals there are multiple sets of rules. Rule-making powers usually rest with the Lord Chancellor or the Secretary of State. They are usually subject to parliamentary procedure, and the Council on Tribunals must be consulted, but there is no standard form or approach, and no statutory requirement to consult stakeholders. In the courts, rules are made by rule committees with judicial and practitioner membership under a unified set of powers, allowing for consistency in the development of procedure. The intention is to replicate this arrangement for the new tribunals.

140.   Section 22 provides for the power to make procedural rules for the new tribunals. Subsection (4) states the overriding objective to be followed by the Tribunal Procedure Committee when it makes Tribunal Procedure Rules. This is similar to the overriding objective governing the Civil Procedure Rules. The purpose of the overriding objective is to ensure that the Tribunal Procedural Committee observes certain fundamental principles when exercising its powers to make procedural rules, such as, securing that justice is done in proceedings before a tribunal and that the tribunal system is accessible and fair.

Schedule 5

141.   Schedule 5 makes provision for (Part 1) what the tribunal procedural rules may contain, (Part 2) the creation of a Tribunal Procedure Committee with responsibility for making such rules, (Part 3) the process for making them and (Part 4) the power to amend primary legislation in pursuance of a rule change. It is expected that the Committee will develop a wide-ranging programme of work.

142.   Part 1 of Schedule 5 sets out matters which may be covered by Tribunal Procedure Rules. It empowers the Tribunal Procedure Committee to make tribunal procedure rules which include provisions in respect of:

- The exercise of concurrent functions (paragraph 2)

- Delegation to staff (paragraph (3)

- Time limits (paragraph 4)

- Repeat applications (paragraph 5)

- The tribunal acting of its own initiative (paragraph 6)

- The extent to which matters may be decided without a hearing and whether a hearing may be public or private (paragraph 7)

- Proceedings without prior notice (paragraph 8)

- Representation (paragraph (9)

- Evidence and witnesses, including provisions relating to the payment of expenses for those attending hearings (paragraph 10)

- Use of information (paragraph 11)

- Costs and expenses (paragraph 12)

- Set–off and interest (paragraph 13)

- Arbitration (paragraph 14)

- Correction of decisions and setting aside of decisions on procedural grounds (paragraph 15)

143.   This is not an exhaustive list and does not limit the broad power in section 22(1) to make procedural rules. Rather, the Tribunal Procedure Committee will exercise its judgement, within the process set out in Part 3 of Schedule 5, to determine which rules are needed in each jurisdiction. It is not intended that each jurisdiction will have rules that cover every aspect listed. Rather the list in Part 1 includes matters which could be considered an extension of the general provisions in section 22.

144.   Paragraph 15, which deals with the correction of decisions and the setting aside of decisions on procedural grounds, does not enable rules to restrict the review powers in sections 9 and 10. Rather, this paragraph allows for rules to allow certain matters to be reviewed otherwise than by a tribunal under sections 9 and 10. For example rules made in reliance on paragraph 15 could provide for a member of staff to correct an accidental error.

145.   Part 2 of Schedule 5 provides for the membership of the Tribunal Procedure Committee. The provisions governing the membership and responsibility for appointing members of the Tribunal Procedure Committee are loosely modelled on those for the rule committees making rules of court but are more flexible because of the diverse nature of tribunals. The Committee is intended to consist of core members and additional members appointed as and when required to provide jurisdiction-specific knowledge.

146. The core membership consists of the Senior President or a person nominated by him, three people with experience of practice in tribunals or giving advice to persons involved in tribunal proceedings, a person nominated by the Administrative Justice and Tribunals Council, a judge from each of the tribunals, a tribunal member and a person with experience in and knowledge of the Scottish legal system. The Lord Chancellor's role is limited to selecting persons with experience of tribunal proceedings or practice and appointing the member selected by the Administrative Justice and Tribunals Council. Consistent with the Concordat, the selection of judicial members falls to either the Lord Chief Justice or the Lord President.

147. Paragraph 24 provides that any additional members are appointed (at the request of the Senior President of Tribunals) by the Lord Chief Justice of England and Wales, the Lord President of the Court of Session or the Lord Chief Justice of Northern Ireland. It is expected that additional members will usually be members of the judiciary. The additional members are intended to bring specialist knowledge to the Committee when discussing particular matters.

148. Under paragraph 25, the Lord Chancellor may make changes to the composition of the Committee, but only with the concurrence of the Lord Chief Justice of England and Wales. The concurrence of the Lord President of the Court of Session or the Lord Chief Justice of Northern Ireland is necessary where such a change would affect a member appointed to the committee by them. The composition of the Tribunal Procedure Committee may need to vary depending on the jurisdiction for which it is making rules and as jurisdictions transfer in.

149. Part 3 of Schedule 5 details the process by which Tribunal Procedure Rules are to be made. This is consistent with the process for making Civil, Family and Criminal Procedure Rules. The Committee is required to consult before rules are made. In order for the rules to be submitted to the Lord Chancellor they must be approved by the Committee. The Lord Chancellor's powers once rules are submitted to him are limited to powers to allow or disallow. However, the Lord Chancellor does have the power to specify a purpose which must be achieved by rules. This is to ensure that, although the Tribunal Procedure Committee is independent, the Lord Chancellor is able to set objectives for the rules.

150. Once allowed by the Lord Chancellor, rules made under this process are subject to negative resolution procedure.

151. Part 4 of Schedule 5 gives the Lord Chancellor power to amend, repeal or revoke any Act in pursuance of a rule change. This power is based upon the provisions in the Civil Procedure Act 1997. An order exercising this power is subject to affirmative resolution procedure. The aim of this provision is to ensure that tribunals operate smoothly and without conflicting with legislation on the statute book.

Section 23: Practice directions

152. Section 23 provides the Senior President with the statutory authority to supplement Tribunal Procedure Rules by means of practice directions. These directions may (for example) take the form of guidance, interpretation of the law, matters of precedent or the delegation of judicial functions to senior members. The giving of practice directions is one of the functions that the Senior President may choose to delegate to Chamber Presidents under section 8. Following the Concordat,

practice directions made either by the Senior President or a Chamber President will usually require the Lord Chancellor's approval. There are two exceptions. The first is where practice directions consist of guidance about the application and interpretation of law or the making of decisions. The second exception is where practice directions consist of criteria for determining which members of the tribunals may be chosen to decide particular categories of matter. Practice directions given by a Chamber President in his own right (i.e. as opposed to directions given by him when exercising, under a delegation, the Senior President's power to give practice directions) will always require the Senior President's approval, whether or not they also require the Lord Chancellor's approval.

Section 24: Mediation

153.   Mediation and other forms of alternative dispute resolution are used increasingly in the justice system. They can provide more efficient and effective remedies, at lower cost and with less pressure on users. Section 24 has been designed to provide the statutory basis for mediation. The use of mediation in tribunal proceedings can be governed both by Tribunal Procedure Rules and by practice directions. It is neither intended nor envisaged that mediation will take place in all jurisdictions, although the term mediation can encompass a broad spectrum of activity. The section will enable staff appointed for the employment tribunals, EAT and AIT, as well as staff appointed for the First-tier and Upper Tribunals, to act as mediators in relation to disputed matters in proceedings before the First-tier or Upper Tribunal.

Section 25: Supplementary powers of Upper Tribunal

154.   Section 25 provides the Upper Tribunal with the powers of the High Court or Court of Session to require the attendance and examination of witnesses and the production and inspection of documents, and all other matters incidental to the Upper Tribunal's functions. These are similar powers to the Employment Appeal Tribunal's powers under section 29 of the Employment Tribunals Act 1996.

Section 26: First-tier Tribunal and Upper Tribunal: sitting places

155.   Section 26 provides for the First-tier Tribunal or the Upper Tribunal to sit anywhere in the United Kingdom irrespective of the law under which a case arises. This will allow the flexible listing of cases for hearing in accordance with the needs of tribunal users. It does not, however, allow a tribunal to decide which law it wants to apply.

Section 27: Enforcement

156.   Subsections (1) to (3) ensure that monetary awards made by the First-tier and Upper Tribunals are enforceable through the courts. These provisions do not alter the methods of enforcement by the courts.

157.   Many tribunal awards in England and Wales are currently enforced through the county court, but there are some where enforcement is currently through the High Court (e.g. the Lands Tribunal where enforcement may be through either court, and the Transport Tribunal where enforcement is in the High Court). Subsection (1) states that a sum payable following a decision of either the First-tier or Upper Tribunal will be recoverable as if it were payable either under an order of a county court in England and Wales or an order of the High Court in England and Wales.

158. Subsection (2) makes corresponding provision for Scotland. An order for payment made as a result of a decision of either the First-tier or Upper Tribunal made in Scotland (or a copy of such an order certified in accordance with Tribunal Procedure Rules) may be enforced as if it were an extract registered decree arbitral bearing a warrant for execution issued by the sheriff court of any sheriffdom in Scotland (i.e. without the intermediate step of registering the decision with the sheriff court).

159. Subsection (3) makes corresponding provision for Northern Ireland. An order for payment made as a result of a decision of either the First-tier or Upper Tribunal in Northern Ireland will be recoverable as if it were payable under either an order of a county court or the High Court in Northern Ireland.

160. Subsection (4) provides that the enforcement provisions in the preceding subsections do not apply to awards of damages, restitution or the recovery of a sum due made to an applicant by the Upper Tribunal exercising its judicial review powers under sections 16(6) or 21(1), because enforcement of such awards is dealt with in sections 16(7) and 21(4).

161. Subsection (5) empowers the Lord Chancellor to make an order (applying to England and Wales or to Northern Ireland) stipulating that a sum of a description specified in the order (payable in pursuance of a decision of the First-tier or Upper Tribunal) may be recoverable as if it were payable either under an order of a county court, or under an order of the High Court, but not both.

162. Subsection (6) allows for Tribunal Procedure Rules to be made which spell out where for the purposes of the enforcement provisions a decision is to be taken to have been made. This is necessary due to the different enforcement methods that apply to Scotland compared with England and Wales. Rules might, for example, provide that where a tribunal is sitting in Scotland to hear a case arising under the law of England and Wales, any sum payable in pursuance of a decision of the tribunal is recoverable as if the decision had been made in England and Wales. Subsection (6) also allows Rules to provide for some sums not to be recoverable under the provisions of the section. This might be appropriate where the particular legislation under which a tribunal is acting contains its own procedures for enforcing awards.

Section 28: Assessors

163. An assessor is an expert who is appointed by a court or tribunal to assist it in dealing with issues within the assessor's area of expertise. Some tribunals already have a power to appoint assessors and this section will allow this practice to continue within the new tribunals. This section provides the First-tier Tribunal or the Upper Tribunal with the power to appoint an assessor to assist where it is dealing with matters that require a special expertise that the tribunal would otherwise not have available to it. This provision will not require an assessor to be used where it is inappropriate to the jurisdiction.

Section 29: Costs or expenses

164. The powers of many tribunals to award costs are currently limited, either because they have no such powers, or because the scope of any power they have is limited. This section grants the tribunals the discretion to order costs and expenses in the same way as courts. It is not intended that these provisions will apply in all jurisdictions, rather that there will be flexibility as part of the creation of the new

system to determine where a costs regime would be appropriate and whether there should be any limits to such a regime (for example, that costs should be awarded only against a party who has acted vexatiously or unreasonably). Subsection (1) is subject to provision made under the Tribunal Procedure Rules so as to allow for such flexibility.

Section 30: Transfer of functions of certain tribunals

165.   The transfer of jurisdictions to the new tribunals is a central feature of the Act. This section provides the Lord Chancellor with the power to transfer jurisdictions from those tribunals listed in the relevant Parts of Schedule 6 to either of the two new tribunals or the employment tribunals or the Employment Appeal Tribunal. In this way adjudicative functions which are currently spread across a wide range of tribunals can be consolidated into the new tribunals and the employment tribunals and Employment Appeal Tribunal.

166.   Subsection (1) empowers the Lord Chancellor to provide for the functions of a tribunal to be transferred to the First-tier Tribunal, Upper Tribunal or the First-tier <u>and</u> Upper Tribunals, with the question as to which of them is to exercise the function in a particular case being determined by a person under provisions of the order or by, or under, Tribunal Procedure Rules. It also provides for the transfer of a function to the First-tier Tribunal to the extent specified in the order, and to the Upper Tribunal to the extent so specified. It provides similarly for transfers to an employment tribunal, or the Employment Appeal Tribunal.

167.   Subsection (3) provides that the Lord Chancellor may further transfer functions in accordance with the provisions of subsection (1).

168.   The general policy of subsections (5) to (8) is to restrict devolved functions from being transferred to the new tribunals.

169.   Under subsection (5), the general rule is that functions of tribunals which are within the legislative competence of the Scottish Parliament or the Northern Ireland Assembly (i.e. devolved) may not be transferred to the First-tier Tribunal or Upper Tribunal under section 30.

170.   Subsections (6) and (7) set out some exceptions. Functions in relation to appeals relating to estate agents and consumer credit, and criminal injury compensation appeals, may be transferred. But transfer of functions relating to criminal injury compensation appeals in Scotland will require the consent of Scottish Ministers.

171.   Subsection (8) provides that if any functions relating to the operation of a tribunal, or expenses for attending the tribunal, are exercisable by the Welsh Ministers, functions of that tribunal may be transferred under section 30 only with the consent of the Welsh Ministers.

Section 31: Transfers under section 30: supplementary powers

172.   Where functions are transferred under section 30, supplementary powers are needed to give the transfer full effect. Subsection (1) confers power on the Lord Chancellor to provide by order for the abolition of a tribunal whose functions have been transferred under section 30.

173.   Orders abolishing tribunals will be brought into force at the point of transfer of their functions (or should the functions of a tribunal be transferred in stages, at the

point of transfer of the last of their functions), thereby removing redundant organisations from statute.

174.   Subsection (2) enables the Lord Chancellor, in transferring functions of a tribunal listed in Schedule 6, to provide for members of the tribunal who are judicial office holders to have a new office within either the First-tier Tribunal or the Upper Tribunal.

175.   Subsection (5) provides that the power under subsection (2) to transfer office-holders into the new tribunals is not available as respects any person whose existing office is that of Commissioner for the General Purposes of Income Tax. That office is abolished by paragraph 1(1) of Schedule 8 to the Act. The offices of General Commissioner of Income Tax and of Clerk to the General Commissioners are expected to be abolished at the point that the functions of the General Commissioners are transferred.

176.   Subsections (7) and (8) allow the Lord Chancellor to provide by order for the continuation of procedural rules following a transfer of functions, if necessary by modification of those rules.

177.   At the point of transfer, orders can be brought into force transferring the existing sets of rules that govern procedure for the tribunals. Minor modifications may be made to the sets of rules where functions are to be transferred to a new tribunal so that they align with the provisions of the Act.

178.   Subsection (9) enables the Lord Chancellor to make, by order, incidental, supplemental, transitional or consequential provision, or provision for savings, to facilitate: a transfer under section 30 of functions of tribunals; the appointment of tribunal judiciary to offices created by the Act; and the transfer of procedural rules.

179.   To facilitate the smooth continuation of tribunal business at and beyond the point of transfer, orders will need to make provision for completion of all work underway in the tribunals at the point of transfer of their functions. The orders will also be able to ensure that references to tribunals that have been abolished are removed from statute.

Section 32: Power to provide for appeal to Upper Tribunal from tribunals in Wales

180.   Where a jurisdiction is exercised by separate tribunals for England and Wales, difficulties could arise if there were different routes of onward appeal for the English and Welsh tribunals.

181.   Section 32 therefore provides for an appeal to the Upper Tribunal from tribunals in Wales in two circumstances. Subsections (1) and (2) deal with a situation where the functions of a tribunal covering both England and Wales are transferred to the First-tier Tribunal in respect of England only. Subsection (3) deals with appeals from tribunals which already have a separate existence in Wales, and which are listed in Part 7 of Schedule 6.

182.   Subsection (2) empowers the Lord Chancellor to provide for appeals from a decision of a tribunal in a Welsh case to be made to the Upper Tribunal instead of to a court. An example of how the power could be used is as follows. An existing tribunal operates in Wales under legislation that is the same as, or corresponds to, the legislation under which the tribunal operates in England. An appeal can be made to a court against decision made by the existing tribunal. The existing tribunal's functions

in England are transferred to the First-tier Tribunal under section 30. When the First-tier Tribunal makes a decision in England under the transferred function, any appeal has to be made not to that court but to the Upper Tribunal. Subsection (2) could be used to provide that when the existing tribunal makes a decision in Wales, an appeal against that decision has to be made not to that court but to the Upper Tribunal.

183.   Subsection (3) empowers the Lord Chancellor to provide for an appeal against a decision of a scheduled tribunal to be made to the Upper Tribunal, where the decision is made by the tribunal in exercising a function in relation to Wales. The power enables an existing right to appeal from the tribunal to a court to be converted into a right to appeal from the tribunal to the Upper Tribunal.

Section 33: Power to provide for appeal to Upper Tribunal from tribunals in Scotland

184.   Where a tribunal jurisdiction is transferred to the new tribunals under section 30, and such a jurisdiction is not transferred in relation to Scotland, section 33 creates a power for the Lord Chancellor to provide (by order) for an appeal to the Upper Tribunal against a corresponding decision made in exercising the untransferred Scottish jurisdiction.

185.   An order under the section provides for the situation where the functions of a tribunal are to be transferred in respect of England, or England and Wales, but not in respect of Scotland; and where there is a right of appeal to the Upper Tribunal from decisions made in exercising the transferred jurisdiction in England, but no right of appeal from the decisions made in exercising the untransferred Scottish jurisdiction.

Section 34: Power to provide for appeal to Upper Tribunal from tribunals in Northern Ireland

186.   Section 34 provides a power (analogous to that provided in section 33 in respect of Scotland) for a new appeal right to the Upper Tribunal from tribunals in Northern Ireland where the equivalent tribunal jurisdiction in England has been transferred (most likely) to the First-tier Tribunal and there is a new appeal right in England to the Upper Tribunal.

Section 35: Transfer of Ministerial responsibilities for certain tribunals

187.   Section 35 makes it possible to transfer to the Lord Chancellor administrative functions of other ministers (and functions of the Commissioners for Her Majesty's Revenue and Customs) in relation to tribunals listed in Schedule 6. The power is similar to the power under section 1 of the Ministers of the Crown Act 1975 which enables transfer of functions between ministers.

188.   Subsections (8) and (9) taken together prevent functions transferred to the Lord Chancellor from being transferred to another Minister of the Crown under subsection (1) or under the Ministers of the Crown Act 1975. This will replicate the effect of section 19 of, and Schedule 7 to, the Constitutional Reform Act 2005, entrenching judiciary-related functions in the office of the Lord Chancellor, and so helping to secure the independence of tribunals from the departments formerly responsible for them.

Section 36: Transfer of powers to make procedural rules for certain tribunals

189.   Section 36 enables the Lord Chancellor by order to transfer power to make procedural rules for certain tribunals to himself or to the Tribunal Procedure Committee.

190.   Most of the powers that may be transferred under this section are currently exercisable by the Secretary of State. This power will allow the Lord Chancellor to:

- standardise the process for making rules for those tribunals whose functions are not scheduled to transfer into the new tribunal structure; or

- cater for the possibility that tribunal rules need to be made before the Tribunal Procedure Committee is operational; or

- transfer the responsibility for making rules for particular tribunals to the Tribunal Procedure Committee before their functions are transferred to the First-tier Tribunal or Upper Tribunal.

191.   The Act as enacted does not confer power to transfer the Secretary of State's power to make procedural rules for the employment tribunals.

Section 37: Power to amend lists of tribunals in Schedule 6

192.   Section 37 gives the Lord Chancellor the power to amend the lists of tribunals in Schedule 6 to the Act by: addition to a list; removal from a list; removing a list from the Schedule; or adding a list of tribunals to the Schedule.

193.   The power is constrained by subsections (2), (3) and (4):

- Under subsection (2)(a), a tribunal created otherwise than by or under an enactment (e.g. a private tribunal of some kind) cannot be brought within the new structure.

- Under subsection (2)(b), tribunals created after the last day of the Session in which the Act is passed (likely to be a day in October/November 2007) may not be added to any of the lists of tribunals in Schedule 6. If the First-tier Tribunal or Upper Tribunal is to have jurisdiction created by later legislation then it will need to be conferred by that later legislation rather than transferred using the machinery of section 30. As the First-tier and Upper Tribunals are all-purpose in nature it is not expected that there will be a need to create any new tribunals.

- Subsections (2)(c) and (3) preserve the position of the Welsh Ministers by requiring the consent of the Welsh Ministers where they have a power in relation to a tribunal.

- Subsection (4) prevents the power being used to bring any of the ordinary courts of law into the new tribunal structure. The terms "tribunal" and "ordinary court of law" are not defined but follow the terminology used in the Tribunals and Inquiries Act 1992.

Schedule 6

194.   Schedule 6 has to be read alongside sections 30 to 36 of the Act. Schedule 6 describes which of sections 30 to 36 apply to the various tribunals listed in the Schedule. There are three main powers that the Lord Chancellor can exercise in relation to the tribunals listed in the Schedule: section 30 deals with the transfer of tribunals' functions, including adjudicative functions; section 35 deals with the transfer of executive functions in relation to tribunals to the Lord Chancellor; and section 36 deals with the transfer of rule making powers to the Lord Chancellor and the Tribunal Procedure Committee.

195.   Because of the number of permutations, Schedule 6 as enacted contains seven lists:

- Part 1: tribunals where all three types of function can be transferred.

- Part 2: tribunals where only the adjudicative and executive functions can be transferred. There are no rule-making powers to transfer.

- Part 3: tribunals where only the adjudicative and rule-making powers can be transferred because all executive functions are already with the Lord Chancellor.

- Part 4: tribunals where only the tribunal's functions can be transferred.

- Part 5: tribunals where executive functions can be transferred to the Lord Chancellor and rule-making functions to the Tribunal Procedure Committee or Lord Chancellor but there can be no transfer of the tribunal's functions.

- Part 6: tribunals where only executive functions can be transferred. No change is intended to the tribunal's functions, and rule-making powers are to remain with the Secretary of State, as indicated in *Transforming Public Services*.

- Part 7: tribunals in Wales where onward appeals can be to the Upper Tribunal instead of the courts.

Section 38: Orders under sections 30-36: supplementary

196.   This section provides for power to amend, repeal or revoke enactments in connection with orders under sections 30 to 36 (i.e. covering the transfer of functions of tribunals; abolition of tribunals; mapping of tribunal judicial office holders to the offices established by the Act; continuation of tribunal procedural rules after transfer of functions; incidental, supplemental, transitional and consequential provisions; appeal routes for tribunals in Wales; appeal routes for tribunals in Scotland; appeal routes for tribunals in Northern Ireland; transfer of ministerial responsibilities for tribunals; transfer of power to make tribunal procedural rules).

Section 39: Administrative support for certain tribunals: The general duty

197.   Section 39 places the Lord Chancellor under a statutory obligation to ensure there is an efficient and effective system of tribunal administration. The duty is framed in respect of the First-tier Tribunal, the Upper Tribunal, the employment tribunals, the Employment Appeal Tribunal and the Asylum and Immigration Tribunal. It mirrors section 1 of the Courts Act 2003, which sets out the Lord Chancellor's duty in respect of the courts in England and Wales. It is intended to show that tribunals are to be treated no less favourably than the courts.

Section 40: Tribunal staff and services and Section 41: Provision of accommodation

198.   Sections 40 and 41 are modelled on sections 2 and 3 of the Courts Act 2003 and grant the Lord Chancellor similar powers to provide staff, services and accommodation for tribunals. Section 40 allows the Lord Chancellor to employ civil servants as tribunal staff, so that he can discharge his duty of administering the tribunals and providing support services.

199.   Subsection (2) enables the Lord Chancellor to contract out certain functions. However, subsection (3) (like section 2 of the Courts Act 2003), prohibits the Lord

Chancellor from contracting out functions which involve making judicial decisions or exercising any judicial discretion.

200.　　　A small number of tribunals listed in Schedule 6 have contracted out some staff functions. Examples include the Lands Tribunal, where some staff functions relating to the maintenance of the Tribunal's library are contracted out; and the AIT, where typing services are contracted out.

201.　　　Where it is decided that administrative functions are best delivered by contracting out, an order will be made under subsection (4) enabling contracts to be signed. Orders will be made only after consultation with the Senior President under subsection (5).

202.　　　Section 41 gives the Lord Chancellor power to provide, equip, maintain and manage tribunal accommodation.

Section 42: Fees

203.　　　Section 42 has been designed to cover in part those tribunals which currently charge a fee for their services and in part the possibility that at some point in the future it may be appropriate to charge fees in other or new jurisdictions.

204.　　　Under subsection (1) the Lord Chancellor will have a power to prescribe, by order, fees to be paid for anything done in the new tribunals, in the Asylum and Immigration Tribunal and in any other statutory tribunal added to the list by order (under subsection (3)), subject to the affirmative resolution procedure. The corresponding power in respect of court fees under section 92 of the Courts Act 2003 can be used to recover running costs of the courts. Similarly, it is considered that the power under section 42 could be used to set fees at a level designed to recover from users of tribunals some or all of the running costs of (or of a part of) the tribunals concerned.

205.　　　Subsection (5) stipulates that before making an order under section 42, the Lord Chancellor must consult the Senior President and the AJTC.

206.　　　Treasury consent will not be required for changes to existing fee levels (subsection (6)). Where a fee is introduced in an area where a fee has not previously been payable, section 49(6)(c) requires that the order is subject to the affirmative resolution procedure. Section 42 also confers power to set fees for the conduct of mediation by tribunals staff appointed under section 40(1) but, since this section establishes the principle of fees being set for this, the negative resolution procedure will be used when setting them.

Section 43: Report by Senior President of Tribunals

207.　　　Section 43 requires the Senior President to give the Lord Chancellor a report on the cases that have come before the First-tier Tribunal and the Upper Tribunal in each year. The report will also cover cases coming before the employment tribunals and the Employment Appeal Tribunal. This provision is intended to support improvement both in the workings of the tribunals and the standard of decision-making and review in cases which come before the tribunals. Section 43 gives the Senior President some flexibility in deciding which matters should be covered in the report, and the Lord Chancellor some flexibility in deciding which matters are a priority for the report.

Sections 44 and 45: The Administrative Justice and Tribunals Council

208.   The existing Council on Tribunals will be replaced by an Administrative Justice and Tribunals Council (AJTC), which is established by section 44 and Schedule 7. The AJTC, like the Council on Tribunals, will be a non-departmental public body, but will have a wider remit.

209.   When the AJTC comes into existence, the Council on Tribunals (and its Scottish Committee) will be abolished. This will be effected by section 45. Section 45 enables the Lord Chancellor to make an order transferring any property, rights or liabilities the Council on Tribunals may have at the time when it is abolished to the new AJTC. The order is to be subject to negative resolution procedure.

Schedule 7: Administrative Justice and Tribunals Council

210.   Schedule 7 makes provision for the AJTC. It is divided into 4 parts.

211.   Part 1 (paragraphs 1 to 11) deals with the membership of the AJTC and for the Committees of the AJTC.

212.   Paragraph 1 provides that the AJTC is to consist of a minimum of 10 and a maximum of 15 members and the Parliamentary Commissioner for Administration. Those members, other than the Parliamentary Commissioner for Administration (who is appointed on an ex-officio basis), are to be appointed by the Scottish Ministers, the Welsh Ministers and the Lord Chancellor, each with the concurrence of the others.

213.   Paragraph 2 makes provision for the nomination of the Chairman of the AJTC. The nomination is of a member of the AJTC and is made by the Lord Chancellor after consulting the Scottish and Welsh Ministers. Paragraph 2 also provides for the terms of office of the Chairman.

214.   Paragraph 3 makes provision for the terms of office for members appointed under paragraph 1. Such members are to hold and leave their office in accordance with the terms on which they have been appointed. The Lord Chancellor may remove an appointed member on the grounds of inability or misbehaviour but this power can only be exercised with the concurrence of the Scottish or Welsh Ministers where the power is being exercised in relation to a person appointed by one of them. Members may resign by writing to the Lord Chancellor or in the case of persons appointed by the Scottish or Welsh Ministers, by writing to those Ministers.

215.   Paragraphs 4 and 7 establish the Scottish and Welsh Committees of the AJTC. Paragraphs 4(2) and 7(2) provide that each Committee is to consist of the Parliamentary Commissioner for Administration, the Public Services Ombudsman for each jurisdiction, the members of the AJTC appointed under paragraph 1(2) by the Scottish or Welsh Ministers as the case may be and a specified number of other persons who are not members of the AJTC appointed by the Scottish or Welsh Ministers under paragraphs 4 and 7 as appropriate.

216.   Paragraphs 6 and 9 provide for the term of office for those members of the Scottish or Welsh Committees who are not members of the AJTC and have been appointed by the Scottish or Welsh Ministers to their respective Committees as described above. Such members are to hold and leave their office in accordance with the terms on which they were appointed and can be removed by the Scottish or Welsh Ministers as appropriate on the ground of inability or misbehaviour. Resignation can be effected by writing to the Scottish or Welsh Ministers as appropriate.

217. Paragraphs 5 and 8 provide for the nomination of the Chairman of the Scottish and Welsh Committees. The relevant Ministers are responsible for nominating a member of the AJTC who is appointed by them to become the Chairman. The terms of office of those Chairmen are provided in paragraphs 5 and 8.

218. Paragraph 10 makes the Lord Chancellor responsible for the remuneration of the members of the AJTC and the Scottish and Welsh Committees.

219. Part 2 of Schedule 7 explains the functions of the AJTC. In summary, the AJTC has functions in relation to the administrative justice system, tribunals and statutory inquiries.

220. Paragraph 13 makes it clear that the AJTC is responsible for keeping the administrative justice system under review. This function extends to the overall system by which decisions of an administrative or executive nature are made in respect of a particular person. The AJTC can advise the Lord Chancellor, the Scottish and Welsh Ministers and the Senior President on the development of the administrative justice system and make such reports as it thinks are necessary in relation to its areas of responsibility under paragraph 13(1).

221. Paragraph 14 explains the AJTC's general functions with respect to tribunals. The AJTC's responsibility is in relation to "listed tribunals" as defined in Part 4 of Schedule 7. Listed tribunals include the First-tier Tribunal, the Upper Tribunal and also any other tribunal that an authority who has responsibility for a tribunal provides is to be a listed tribunal for the purpose of Schedule 7. So the AJTC's responsibility for tribunals may extend to tribunals other than the First-tier and Upper Tribunals. By virtue of paragraph 14 the AJTC is to keep listed tribunals under review and report on those tribunals and also on any matter that the AJTC thinks is of special importance. The AJTC is also to consider and report on any matter referred to it jointly by the Lord Chancellor, Scottish Ministers and Welsh Ministers under paragraph 16. The AJTC may also scrutinise and comment on legislation that is extant or proposed, including procedural rules, relating to tribunals.

222. Paragraph 15 documents the AJTC's duties in respect of statutory inquiries. The AJTC's duties involve keeping statutory inquiries under review, reporting on them and reporting on other matters it determines to be of particular importance. As with tribunals it must also consider and report on any matter referred to it by the Lord Chancellor, the Welsh Ministers and the Scottish Ministers jointly under paragraph 16.

223. Paragraph 17 makes provision for the procedure to be followed when the AJTC makes a report in relation to its functions in respect of tribunals under paragraph 14 and statutory inquiries under paragraph 15.

224. Paragraphs 18 and 19 ensure that the Scottish and Welsh Committees are consulted on any matter that relates solely to their jurisdiction before the Council is authorised to report on it. These paragraphs also provide that the Scottish and Welsh Committees can make reports to the AJTC on their own motion in relation to matters specified in paragraphs 18 and 19. If the AJTC does not make a report on a matter dealt with in a report made to it by the Scottish or Welsh Committee or in making a report the AJTC does not adopt the Committee's reports without modification, the Committee can submit its report to the Scottish or Welsh Ministers as the case may be. The Scottish and Welsh Ministers must lay reports submitted to them in these

circumstances before the Scottish Parliament or the National Assembly for Wales as appropriate.

225. Paragraph 21 sets out the AJTC's duty to make an annual report on its proceedings and the corresponding duty on the Scottish Committee and Welsh Committee. The AJTC's report must be laid before Parliament and also before the Scottish Parliament and National Assembly for Wales. The reports of the Scottish and Welsh Committees under this paragraph must be laid before the Scottish Parliament and National Assembly for Wales respectively.

226. Paragraph 22 makes provision for members of the AJTC, the Scottish Committee and the Welsh Committee to attend proceedings of a listed tribunal (as defined in Part 4 of Schedule 7) or statutory inquiry as observers even when those proceedings are held in private or do not take the form of a hearing. This right is subject to any statutory provision that expressly excludes these members from proceedings.

227. Paragraph 23 provides for the application of certain provisions in Schedule 7 to Northern Ireland.

228. Part 3 of Schedule 7 provides for the AJTC to be consulted on procedural rules for a listed tribunal (as defined in Part 4 of Schedule 7).

229. Paragraph 24(2) excludes rules made or to be made by the Tribunal Procedural Committee in relation to a listed tribunal from the general duty in paragraph 24(1). The duty in paragraph 24(1) is for a Minister of the Crown, a Scottish Minister or a Welsh Minister to consult the AJTC before it takes any action outlined in that paragraph in relation to procedural rules for a listed tribunal (as defined in Part 4 of Schedule 7). This is not necessary in the excluded cases since a member of the AJTC will sit on the Tribunal Procedural Committee.

230. Part 4 contains definitions of terms that apply to Schedule 7, including the definition of "listed tribunal" which means the First-tier Tribunal, the Upper Tribunal or any tribunal that the Lord Chancellor, Scottish Ministers or Welsh ministers requests to be listed for the purpose of Schedule 7 in accordance with paragraph 25(2) of Schedule 7.

231. The power in paragraph 25(2) will enable the oversight responsibilities of the Council to cover tribunals inside and outside the new tribunal system.

Section 46: Delegation of Functions by the Lord Chief Justice etc

232. Section 46 enables the Lord Chief Justice to nominate a judicial office holder (as defined in section 109(4) of the Constitutional Reform Act 2005) to exercise any of the listed functions given to him under the Act. These are:

- Concurrence with the removal of a judge or other member of the First-tier Tribunal from office (Schedule 2 paragraph 3(4)).

- Concurrence with a request for a court judge to sit in the First-tier Tribunal (Schedule 2 paragraph 6(3)(a)).

- Concurrence in the removal of a judge or other member of the Upper Tribunal from office (Schedule 3 paragraph 3(4)).

- Concurrence with a request for a court judge to sit in the Upper Tribunal (Schedule 3 paragraph 6(3)(a)).

- Power to nominate an ordinary judge of the Court of Appeal or a puisne judge of the High Court to preside over a chamber (Schedule 4 paragraph 2(2)).

- Power to nominate an ordinary judge of the Court of Appeal or a puisne judge of the High Court to act as a deputy chamber president (Schedule 4 paragraph 5(5)).

- Consultation on the Lord Chancellor's appointees to the Tribunal Procedure Committee (Schedule 5, paragraph 21(2)).

- Power to appoint members to the Tribunal Procedure Committee (Schedule 5 paragraphs 22 and 24).

- Concurrence in an order changing the composition of the Tribunal Procedure Committee (Schedule 5 paragraph 25).

233.   This section also makes similar provision for the Lord President of the Court of Session and the Lord Chief Justice of Northern Ireland.

Section 47: Co-operation in relation to judicial training, guidance and welfare

234.   Section 47 establishes a duty of co-operation between the offices of the Senior President of Tribunals, the Lord Chief Justices and the Lord President in relation to judicial guidance, training and welfare.   The Senior President has responsibility for the maintenance of appropriate arrangements for the welfare, training and guidance of tribunal judiciary and members of the First-tier and Upper Tribunals (paragraph 8 of Schedule 2 and paragraph 9 of Schedule 3) and for judiciary and members of the employment tribunals, the EAT and the AIT (paragraphs 40, 44 and 54 of Schedule 8). The Lord Chief Justices of England and Wales and Northern Ireland have the same responsibility for the court judiciary.

235.   In carrying out these responsibilities it is desirable for there to be a duty of co-operation between the Senior President and the Lord Chief Justices (and including the Lord President even though he has no statutory responsibility for such provision at the time of Royal Assent to this Act). In practical terms, this means the use by tribunals of institutions which report to the Lord Chief Justice of England and Wales (e.g. the Judicial Studies Board for training, the Judicial Communications Office for advice on media and handling, and arrangements for counselling and supporting judges under the contract that was set up by MoJ and are now the responsibility of the Judicial Office).

Section 48: Consequential and other amendments, and transitional provisions

236.   Section 48 gives effect to Schedule 8 (consequential and other amendments) and to Schedule 9 (transitional provisions).

Schedule 8

237.   Paragraph 1 abolishes the office of General Commissioner (styled in legislation as "Commissioner for the general purposes of income tax") and the offices of clerk, and assistant clerk, to any General Commissioner. The General Commissioners hear appeals brought under the Taxes Management Act 1970. The General Commissioners must appoint a clerk and if necessary an assistant clerk to

provide administrative functions and legal advice to the General Commissioners. Provision is made for the General Commissioners by section 2 of the Taxes Management Act 1970 and the clerks by section 3. This paragraph is expected to be brought into force when the functions of the General Commissioners are transferred to the new Tribunals. It is not intended to use the power under section 31(2) so as to cause a person holding the office of General Commissioner to become a transferred-in judge of the new Tribunals.

238.   Paragraphs 2, 8, 15, 17 to 19, 24, 28, 30, 32, 33, 53, 56 to 58, 60 and 61 amend references or provisions concerning the "Council on Tribunals". These amendments reflect the provisions in section 44 and Schedule 7 establishing the Administrative Justice and Tribunals Council and section 45 abolishing the Council on Tribunals.

239.   Paragraphs 3, 9 to 12, 22, 49 to 52 and 59 enable certain hearings or inquiries to constitute a statutory inquiry for the purposes of the Administrative Justice and Tribunals Council's functions with respect to statutory inquiries under paragraph 15 of Schedule 7.

240.   Paragraphs 4 and 5 will ensure that members of bodies established by the Act are disqualified from sitting in the House of Commons or the Northern Ireland Assembly.

241.   Paragraph 6 enables litigants in person to obtain costs and expenses under the 1975 Act in proceedings before the First-tier Tribunal or Upper Tribunal where costs are awarded. Paragraph 6 also amends section 1(4) of the 1975 Act to provide that the definition of "rules of court" in that section, in relation to the First-tier and Upper Tribunal, means Tribunal Procedural Rules.

242.   Paragraph 7 makes the Administrative Justice and Tribunals Council ("AJTC") and the Scottish and Welsh Committees of the AJTC subject to the statutory duty under section 71 of the Race Relations Act 1976 so when carrying out their functions they have to have regard to the need to eliminate unlawful discrimination and to promote equal opportunity and good relations.

243.   Paragraph 13 amends sections 26(2)(e) and 37(2) of the Food Safety Act 1990. The amendments to section 26(2)(e) allow regulations to be made to provide for appeals to the First-tier Tribunal or Upper Tribunal. Amendments to section 37(2) ensure that section 37(1)(c) (appeals to the magistrates or sheriff court) does not apply when regulations provide for an appeal to a Tribunal constituted in accordance with the regulations or to the First-tier or Upper Tribunal.

244.   Paragraph 16 ensures that judges and other members of the First-tier and Upper Tribunal are banned under section 75 of the Courts and Legal Services Act 1990 from practising as lawyers.

245.   Paragraph 25 removes the requirement for the chairman of certain tribunals to be selected by the appropriate authority from a panel appointed by the Lord Chancellor.

246.   Paragraphs 26 and 27 will not be commenced at the same time. Paragraph 26 allows for an interim period where there will be some rules being made by Ministers etc and some by the Tribunal Procedure Committee. When all rules are being made by the Tribunal Procedure Committee paragraph 27 can be commenced to remove section 8 of the 1992 Act as that provision will no longer be necessary.

247.   Paragraph 29 amends section 14(1) of the 1992 Act so the definition is only applicable to decisions. This is consequential on the repeal by the Act of the provisions of the 1992 Act (sections 1, 4 and 8) that contain references to the working of tribunals or their procedural rules.

248.   Paragraph 31 allows for judicial offices created under the Act to be become qualifying and relevant offices for the respective purposes of pension and retirement provisions under the Judicial Pensions and Retirement Act 1993 ('the 1993 Act'). This paragraph therefore has to be read in conjunction with the provisions of the 1993 Act. Part 1 of the 1993 Act provides that a person who retires from a qualifying judicial office is entitled, subject to certain conditions, to a judicial pension under the 1993 Act. A "qualifying judicial office" is defined in section 1(6) of the 1993 Act as being that of a person who holds, on a salaried basis, any one or more of the offices specified in Schedule 1 to the 1993 Act. Any reference in the 1993 Act to a "qualifying judicial office" is a reference to any office so specified if it is held on a salaried basis. So, the entitlement of any judge or other member of the First-tier Tribunal or the Upper Tribunal to a judicial pension under the 1993 Act depends on whether or not they hold their office on a salaried as opposed to fee paid basis. This should be borne in mind when considering the application of the provisions of paragraph 31 in relation to the entitlement of judges and other members of the new Tribunals to a judicial pension.

249.   Paragraph 34 makes provision for oaths to be taken by Criminal Injuries Compensation Panel adjudicators (to mirror provisions for the First–tier and Upper tribunal judges). CICAP adjudicators are not included in the general oath taking provisions of Schedule 2.

250.   Paragraphs 35 to 48, in addition to amending existing provisions of the Employment Tribunals Act 1996, insert a number of new sections to ensure that certain provisions of the Act relating to the judges and other members of the First-tier and Upper Tribunal are replicated in the legislation applying to employment tribunals and the Employment Appeal Tribunal (paragraph 54 makes similar amendments to the Nationality, Immigration and Asylum Act 1992 for Asylum and Immigration Tribunal office holders).   The changes are required as, while the employment tribunals and the Employment Appeal Tribunal are not part of the First-tier and Upper Tribunals, they are intended to benefit from being administratively a part of the Tribunals Service.

251.   Paragraph 36 confers the title of Employment Judge on members of a panel of chairmen of employment tribunals.

252.   Paragraph 38 requires the Secretary of State to act jointly with the Lord Chancellor when exercising certain powers to amend provisions in that Act.

253.   Paragraphs 40 and 44 make the Senior President of Tribunals responsible for the training, welfare and guidance of members of employment tribunals and members of the Employment Appeal Tribunal, in the same way that he is for members of the First-tier Tribunal and Upper Tribunal (under paragraph 8 of Schedule 2 and paragraph 9 of Schedule 3).

254.   Paragraph 41 confers power to make practice directions in relation to employment tribunals on the Senior President and requires the consent of the Senior

President and the Lord Chancellor for practice directions made by Presidents of
Employment Tribunals.

255.   Paragraph 42 makes provision for mediation in employment tribunals on a
similar basis to section 24 (mediation); the major difference being that ACAS must be
consulted before making a practice direction for mediation in employment tribunals.

256.   Paragraph 43 amends section 15(1) of the Employment Tribunals Act 1996
(enforcement in England and Wales as an order of a county court) so that an unpaid
employment tribunal award does not need to be registered in the county court before
enforcement can take place. This mirrors provisions in relation to the First-tier
Tribunal and the Upper Tribunal in section 27 (enforcement).

257.   Paragraph 47 makes additional provision for practice directions about the
procedure of the Employment Appeal Tribunal to be given by the Senior President of
Tribunals or the President of the Employment Appeals Tribunal.

258.   Paragraph 54, in addition to amending existing provisions of the Nationality,
Immigration and Asylum Act 2002, inserts a number of new sections to ensure that
certain provisions of that Act relating to the judges and other members of the First-tier
and Upper Tribunal are replicated in the legislation applying for the Asylum and
Immigration Tribunal and that certain responsibilities of the Lord Chancellor and the
Senior President extend to its members. These amendments ensure that certain
judicial leadership powers in the Act that apply to the First-tier and Upper Tribunal
are replicated for the Asylum and Immigration Tribunal. This reflects the intention of
the Act to provide coherent judicial leadership and administrative support to all
tribunals that form part of the Tribunal Service even though they may not be within
the First-tier and Upper Tribunals.

259.   Section 107 of the 2002 Act has been amended to ensure that the Senior
President of Tribunals may give practice directions to the Asylum and Immigration
Tribunal after having obtained the approval of the Lord Chancellor. Also for any
directions given by the President of the Asylum and Immigration Tribunal to be given
with the approval of the Senior President of Tribunals and the Lord Chancellor. The
requirements for approval in both instances are subject to qualifications (in the same
way as are parallel provisions for the First-tier and Upper Tribunals and employment
tribunals and Employment Appeal Tribunal).

260.   Schedule 4 to the 2002 Act, which provides for the membership of the Asylum
and Immigration Tribunal and related matters, is amended to make provision for: the
concurrence of the relevant Lord Chief Justice on removal as a member of the Asylum
and Immigration Tribunal; in assignment of members of other tribunals by the Senior
President with consent of the President of the Asylum and Immigration Tribunal; the
Senior President to be responsible for the training, guidance and welfare of members
of the Asylum and Immigration Tribunal; and the taking of oaths of persons appointed
under Schedule 4 who have not previously taken the required oaths after accepting
another office.

261.   Paragraph 55 amends section 98 of the Courts Act 2003 (register of judgments
and orders etc) so that monetary decisions or awards of the First-tier Tribunal, the
Upper Tribunal, an Employment Tribunal, or the Employment Appeal Tribunal may
be included on the Register of Judgments and Orders established under the 2003 Act.
Inclusion on the Register, which is often consulted by banks, building societies, credit

companies etc when considering applications for credit, may make it more difficult for defaulters to obtain credit (and thus provides an incentive to pay the sum due).

262.　　Paragraphs 62 to 66 amend the Constitutional Reform Act 2005. Section 109(5) is amended to ensure that the Senior President of Tribunals is included as a senior judge for the purpose of the disciplinary powers of the Lord Chief Justice in section 108 of that Act. Schedule 7 is amended so that references to the Tribunals and Inquiries Act 1992 are removed. In Schedule 12, a new sub-paragraph (2A) is inserted into paragraph 2 to allow certain office holders belonging to the new Tribunals to join the list of those who may be members of the Judicial Appointments Commission. Finally, Schedule 14 is amended so that judges and other members who are to be appointed under the Act by the Lord Chancellor (or, in the case of judges of the Upper Tribunal, by Her Majesty on recommendation of the Lord Chancellor) are selected by the Judicial Appointments Commission. Such selection will not apply to the transfer in of members of existing tribunals under section 31(2) or to appointments that fall to be made by a senior judge.

Schedule 9

263.　　Schedule 9 sets out a number of transitional provisions, including provisions relating to the retirement dates and pensions for judges and other members of the First-tier Tribunal and Upper Tribunal. Much of Schedule 9 therefore has to be read in conjunction with the specific provisions of the Judicial Pensions and Retirement Act 1993 ('the 1993 Act') and in particular Part 1 of that Act. Part 1 of the 1993 Act provides that a person who holds qualifying judicial office is entitled to a judicial pension under the 1993 Act. A "qualifying judicial office" is defined in section 1(6) of the 1993 Act as being that of a person who holds, on a salaried basis, any one or more of the offices specified in Schedule 1 to the 1993 Act. Any reference in the 1993 Act to a "qualifying judicial office" is a reference to any office so specified if it is held on a salaried basis. So, the entitlement of any judge or other member of the First-tier Tribunal or the Upper Tribunal to a judicial pension under the 1993 Act depends on whether or not they hold their office on a salaried as opposed to fee paid basis. This should be borne in mind when considering the application of the provisions of Schedule 9 in relation to the entitlement of judges and other members of the new Tribunals to a judicial pension. Schedule 9 is divided into 4 Parts.

Part 1 (General and Miscellaneous)

264.　　Paragraph 1 explains that the specific provisions in Schedule 9 are not to be taken to prejudice:

- the power of the Lord Chancellor under section 31(9), in connection with the provisions of section 30 (transfer of functions of certain Tribunals) and the preceding parts of section 31 (transfers under section 30: supplementary powers), to make transitional (and other) provision; or

- the power of the Lord Chancellor (or Secretary of State in relation to Chapter 3 of Part 5) to make such transitional etc. provision by order as he considers necessary or expedient to give full effect to any provision of the Act.

265.　　Paragraph 2 makes provision for the Lord Chancellor to make an order which allows a member of a tribunal listed in any of Parts 1 to 4 of Schedule 6 to the Act to be treated as a person whom the Lord Chief Justice can appoint to the Tribunal Procedure Committee.

266.　　　This will allow the Lord Chief Justice to appoint to that Committee a person belonging to a particular tribunal before that tribunal has been fully transferred into the new system. These provisions will allow the formation of a Committee from existing tribunals in anticipation of their transfer, and before they can be formally part of the Tribunal Procedure Committee so that preparatory work can be undertaken.

267.　　　Part 2 (Judges and other members of First-tier and Upper Tribunals: Retirement dates)

268.　　　Part 2 of Schedule 9 provides for the retirement age of judges and other members who are to transfer into or are appointed to the First-tier or Upper Tribunal and who have a pre-existing right to retire at an age other than that provided by section 26(1) of the 1993 Act.

269.　　　Paragraph 5 makes provision for the retirement date that is to apply to judges and other members of the First-tier and Upper Tribunal who, in relation to an existing office, either have personal retirement dates that are later than 70, or do not have to retire at any specified time. Paragraph 5 provides that such persons are subject to the provisions of section 26(1) of the 1993 Act as if it provided in the former case above for that person to vacate his office on his personal retirement date and in the latter case above for that person to vacate his office on the date provided for at paragraph 7 of the Schedule rather than at the age otherwise provided by that section. Section 26(1) of the 1993 Act provides that a person holding any of the offices for the time being specified in Schedule 5 to that Act (a "relevant office") shall vacate that office on the day on which he attains the age of 70 or such lower age as may for the time being be specified for the purpose. So, paragraph 5 protects the position of judges or other members who before becoming judges or other members of the First-tier or Upper Tribunal hold offices allowing them to retire later than age 70. Paragraph 5 applies to the situations defined in paragraphs 6 and 7 respectively - where a person has a compulsory retirement age later than 70 or, in the defined circumstances, no retirement age at all. Paragraph 5 is however subject to the provisions of paragraph 8 described below.

270.　　　Paragraph 8 makes special provision for a judge or other member of the First-tier or Upper Tribunal who would be covered by the provisions in paragraph 5 due to having held an office with a retirement date other than that provided in section 26(1) of the 1993 Act but who also by virtue of having held a judicial office on the 30th March 1995 falls under Schedule 7 of the 1993 Act (retirement dates: transitional provisions). Schedule 7 allows such persons to retire at a "potential retirement date" rather than the date otherwise stipulated in section 26(1). Paragraph 8 deals with the interaction of both paragraph 5 of this Schedule and Schedule 7 to the 1993 Act, so that a person otherwise falling within both paragraph 5 and Schedule 7 can only benefit from the provision under paragraph 5 if, by virtue of the office in question, he has a protected retirement date under that paragraph which is later than his potential retirement date under Schedule 7.

271.　　　Paragraph 9 makes provision for a person holding an office in a tribunal listed in Schedule 6 to the Act who has a retirement date for that office that is later than the age of 70. Paragraph 9 provides that the fact that the person has attained the age of 70 will not make him ineligible for appointment or re-appointment to the relevant judicial office as defined in paragraph 3 of Schedule 9 provided he has not yet reached the date on which he is required to vacate the office in the listed tribunal.

Part 3 (judges and other members of First-tier and Upper Tribunals: Pensions where office acquired under section 31(2))

272.   Part 3 of Schedule 9 makes transitional provision about the right of transferred-in judges and other members of the First-tier and Upper Tribunal either to remain in their pre-existing pension schemes or to opt-in to Part 1 of the Judicial Pensions and Retirement Act 1993 ('the 1993 Act'). Part 1 of the 1993 Act deals with entitlement to pension benefits under the 1993 Act in respect of persons holding a qualifying judicial office listed in Schedule 1 to that Act.

273.   Paragraph 11 provides that, in the prescribed circumstances, and subject to paragraph 12, a judge can choose that the provisions affording a judicial pension under Part 1 of the 1993 Act apply. The provisions of Part 1 of the 1993 Act which would otherwise cause the person automatically to fall within that Part are disapplied. But, paragraph 11 makes provision for transferred-in judges and other members of the new Tribunals to opt-into the scheme of the 1993 Act and thus not to remain outside of that scheme in their pre-existing pension scheme.

274.   Paragraph 12 has to be read alongside the provisions of paragraph 11. Paragraph 12 provides for the Lord Chancellor to make regulations prescribing the circumstances under which an opt-in election under paragraph 11 (for Part 1 of the 1993 Act to apply) may be made.

275.   Paragraph 13 allows that in default of an option under paragraph 11, a person's service in their new office under the Act will be subject to the public service pension scheme they belonged to before transferring to the new office, in the same way as before they had transferred.

Part 4 (amendments to the Judicial Pensions and Retirement Act 1993)

276.   Paragraph 15 amends section 1 of the 1993 Act by inserting a new paragraph (e) into subsection (1) so that section 1 now applies Part 1 (arrangements for judicial pensions) to transferred–in judges and other members of the First-tier and Upper Tribunal who are subsequently appointed to a different judicial office.

277.   Paragraphs 16, 17 and 18 ensure that transferred-in judges and other members of the First-tier and the Upper Tribunal to whom Part 1 of the 1993 Act becomes applicable are subject to the rights and requirements of the 1993 Act scheme rather than any previous pension scheme they belonged to.

278.   Paragraph 16 makes provision for section 9(4) of the 1993 Act (contribution towards costs of surviving spouse's, surviving civil partner's and surviving children's pension) to apply.

279.   Paragraph 17 makes provision in section 12(1) of the 1993 Act for transferred-in judges and other members who opt for Part 1 of the 1993 Act to apply to them, or to whom the 1993 Act comes to apply automatically, to have accrued rights to benefit under a judicial pension scheme other than that in the 1993 Act transferred to the scheme under Part 1 of the 1993 Act.

280.   Paragraph 18 inserts a new section into the 1993 Act (section 12A) which makes provision for transferred-in judges and other members who opt to have Part 1 of the Act apply to them (or to whom it comes to apply automatically) to have any accrued rights under a civil service pension scheme transferred to the scheme under Part 1 of the Act. When the rights under the civil service pension scheme are

transferred it will no longer have effect in relation to the transferred-in judge or other member and no pension benefits will be paid to that person under that scheme. The provisions of section 12A added by this paragraph also enable regulations to be made for calculating and prescribing the manner in which the transferred rights are to be given effect under Part 1 of the 1993 Act. Paragraph 18 also inserts a new section 12B, which provides for the determination of entitlement to, and the rate or amount of benefits under the 1993 Act scheme, where accrued pension rights have been transferred under section 12 or 12A of the 1993 Act. Paragraph 19 ensures that Schedule 2 (transfer of accrued benefits) to the 1993 Act does not apply to transfers under section 12A, in the same way as it does not apply to transfers under section 12 of that Act.

Section 49: Orders and regulations under Part 1: supplemental and procedural provisions

281.   Section 49 sets out the procedure to be followed in respect of the various types of order which can be made under Part 1. These powers are mostly exercisable by the Lord Chancellor. The Scottish Ministers and the Welsh Ministers can make orders adding tribunals administered by them to the listed tribunals which the AJTC reviews and reports on (Schedule 7, paragraph 25(2)). Under section 7(9) the Senior President can make an order relating to the jurisdictions assigned to chambers, and section 49(2) provides that this order is to be treated as if it had been made by a Minister of the Crown.

Under subsection (6) orders under the following provisions are subject to affirmative resolution:

- Section 11(8): power to determine who is to be treated as a party to a case for the purposes of a right of appeal to the Upper Tribunal;

- Section 13(6): restrictions on right of appeal to the Court of Appeal;

- Section 13(14): power to determine who is to be treated as a party to a case for the purposes of a right of appeal to the Court of Appeal;

- Section 30: power to transfer functions of a tribunal into the new tribunal structure;

- Section 31(1): power to abolish tribunals when their functions have been transferred;

- Section 31(2), (7) and (9) and paragraph 30(1) of Schedule 5: but only if the order amends primary legislation;

- Section 32: power to provide for appeals to the Upper Tribunal from tribunals in Wales;

- Section 33: power to provide for appeals to the Upper Tribunal from tribunals in Scotland;

- Section 34: power to provide for appeals to the Upper Tribunal from tribunals in Northern Ireland;

- Section 35: transfer of Ministerial responsibilities to the Lord Chancellor;

- Section 36: transfer of powers to make procedural rules;

- Section 37: power to amend the lists of tribunals in Schedule 6;

- Section 42(1)(a) to (d): fee orders, if no fee has previously been payable (except in the case of fees for mediation by tribunal staff);

- Section 42(3): power to add a tribunal to the list of tribunals to which fees may be prescribed;

- Paragraph 15 of Schedule 4: power to determine composition of tribunals.

282.   All other orders under Part 1 of the Act are to be made by the negative resolution procedure.

PART 2: JUDICIAL APPOINTMENTS

SUMMARY

283.   Part 2 of the Act amends the minimum eligibility requirements for judicial appointments in England and Wales (and for some posts where the office-holders may sit in Scotland or Northern Ireland) with the aim of increasing the diversity of the judiciary. The existing eligibility requirements for judicial office are replaced with the requirement that a person must satisfy the "judicial-appointment eligibility condition". The sections mean that rather than eligibility for office being based on possession of rights of audience for a specified period, a person who wishes to apply for an office under any of the provisions amended by Schedule 10 to the Act will have to show that he has possessed a relevant legal qualification for the requisite period and that while holding that qualification he has been gaining legal experience. In respect of many of the offices, the number of years for which a person must have held his qualification before he becomes eligible for judicial office is also reduced.

284.   Part 2 also enables the Lord Chancellor, following consultation with the Lord Chief Justice and the JAC, to extend by order the list of relevant qualifications for the purpose of the judicial-appointment eligibility condition. This will enable those with relevant qualifications and legal experience to apply for certain offices, which will also be specified in the order.

285.   Part 2 of the Act also makes provision for the appointment to fee-paid judicial office of those who have previously held corresponding salaried appointments (section 53) and makes provision (sections 56 and 57) about appointments (in the civil courts in England and Wales) of district judges, deputy district judges and deputy, and temporary, masters and registrars. Section 58 makes provision about appointments of temporary assistants to the Judge Advocate General, section 59 makes provision about appointments to certain Appeals Commissions, section 60 makes provision about appointment as chairman of the Law Commission and section 61 relates to the Northern Ireland Judicial Appointments Commission.

BACKGROUND

286.   Eligibility for appointment to professional judicial office in England and Wales is currently dependent upon applicants possessing particular qualifications (within the meaning of the Courts and Legal Services Act 1990), which are based on possession of "rights of audience" for a prescribed number of years. The precise category of rights of audience required, and the length of time for which they must have been held, vary according to the judicial office concerned. However, the

practical effect of the current arrangements is to restrict eligibility for almost all judicial posts to persons who have been qualified as barristers or solicitors in England and Wales for at least seven years (or, for some posts, 10 years). (Barristers, advocates and solicitors who have been qualified in Scotland or Northern Ireland for the required number of years are also eligible for some posts, notably in those tribunals which exercise UK-wide jurisdiction).

287.   A consultation paper, Increasing Diversity in the Judiciary, published by the Department for Constitutional Affairs (now the Ministry of Justice) in October 2004, invited views as to whether these statutory eligibility requirements constituted an obstacle to greater diversity in the judiciary. Responses to consultation indicated that the eligibility requirements were considered an obstacle to greater diversity in several respects. First, because they depended on possession of rights of audience before the courts, they helped to foster the (inaccurate) perception that advocacy experience was a requirement for judicial appointment, deterring eligible individuals from applying. Second, they excluded entirely members of certain legal professional groups (for example, legal executives) who might possess the skills, knowledge and experience needed to perform well in judicial office, and who also tended to be drawn from a wider range of backgrounds than barristers and solicitors. It was also argued that the existing requirements were unsatisfactory in that someone who qualified as a barrister or a solicitor but who then did no more legal work of any kind still became eligible for judicial appointment on the seventh anniversary of their qualification. Finally, respondents considered that the periods of time for which a qualification must have been held were too long, disadvantaging those who had joined the profession later in life but whose career paths might nevertheless render them fitted for consideration.

288.   The provisions in this Part of the Act seek to address these concerns by removing the existing link between eligibility for judicial appointment and possession of advocacy rights; by providing for the extension of eligibility for some appropriate appointments to holders of legal qualifications other than barristers and solicitors; by introducing a requirement that a person with a relevant qualification must also have gained legal experience to be eligible for office; and by reducing the number of years for which it is necessary to have held the relevant qualification and gained legal experience. It is to be noted that these changes attach to the eligibility threshold for appointment. The aim is to increase the pool of those eligible for office, but the current system of merit-based appointment will remain. These changes apply to offices under provisions amended by Schedule 10 to the Act, which includes a wide range of judicial offices in both mainstream courts and tribunals.

COMMENTARY ON SECTIONS: PART 2

Section 50: Judicial appointments: "judicial-appointment eligibility condition"

289.   This section sets out the new basis of eligibility for judicial appointment. In order to satisfy the "judicial-appointment eligibility condition", an individual has to hold a "relevant qualification" (i.e. as a barrister, a solicitor or a holder of another specified legal qualification) for a specified minimum number of years (generally five or seven, in place of the seven or ten specified in existing legislation), and has to have gained experience in law for the specified minimum number of years, while holding a relevant qualification. Activities which count as gaining experience in law are set out in section 52.

290.   The section removes the anomaly identified under current legislation whereby an individual who qualifies as a barrister or a solicitor becomes eligible for judicial appointment simply through the passage of time, without necessarily ever having engaged in legal practice following qualification.

Schedule 10: Amendments relating to judicial appointments

291.   The minimum eligibility requirements for judicial offices are contained in a large number of statutory provisions. This Schedule amends those provisions in two main respects. First, the existing requirement of a qualification within the meaning of section 71 of the Courts and Legal Services Act 1990 is replaced by a requirement to satisfy the judicial-appointment eligibility condition on an N-year basis. Second, the period of time for which a qualification should have been held, and experience in law acquired (N years), is reduced. For those judicial appointments which currently require possession of a ten-year qualification under the 1990 Act, the period is reduced to seven years and for those appointments which currently require a seven-year qualification, the period is reduced to five years. Where those with Scottish or Northern Irish qualifications are eligible for appointment, corresponding reductions are made.

Section 51: "Relevant qualification" in section 50: further provision

292.   This section empowers the Lord Chancellor (after consultation with the Lord Chief Justice and the JAC) to extend the list of relevant qualifications for the purpose of the judicial-appointment eligibility condition in section 50. The power is exercisable by order made under the affirmative resolution procedure.

293.   Orders made under this section would say which qualifications – other than being a barrister or a solicitor – would be "relevant qualifications" for the purpose of eligibility for particular judicial offices. The only qualifications which it would be permitted to specify in this way would be those awarded by the Institute of Legal Executives or by other bodies authorised to confer rights of audience or rights to conduct litigation under sections 27 and 28 of the Courts and Legal Services Act 1990. This would provide assurance that the bodies concerned had in place approved training and qualification arrangements for their members. The section also provides for a qualification to cease to be relevant if the body which awarded it ceases to be an authorised body under the procedure set down in the 1990 Act. The Legal Services Bill currently (i.e. Summer 2007) before Parliament would, if enacted in its current form, amend the references to the 1990 Act that are contained in this section.

294.   It is envisaged that the power given to the Lord Chancellor under this section will be exercised in the first instance to extend eligibility for specified appointments to Fellows of the Institute of Legal Executives and to registered patents agents and trade mark attorneys. It also provides flexibility to extend eligibility to duly qualified members of other authorised bodies, should that become appropriate as a result of future developments in the legal profession.

Section 52: Meaning of "gain experience in law" in Section 50

295.   This section defines various ways in which an individual may gain post-qualification experience in law so as to satisfy the "qualifying period" element of the judicial-appointment eligibility condition in section 50. Consistent with the aim of encouraging applications from a wide range of suitably qualified people, these include not only those activities traditionally regarded as part of a lawyer's practice (e.g. legal

advice and assistance) but also exercising judicial functions in a court or tribunal, arbitration and teaching or researching law. Broadly similar activities are also included. Such work need not be performed full-time or for remuneration.

296.   It should be noted that at the same time as gaining experience by undertaking these activities, an individual must also possess a "relevant qualification" – i.e. as a barrister, a solicitor or as a holder of a qualification awarded by one of the bodies to be specified by order under section 51.

Section 53: Transfer from salaried to fee-paid judicial office

297.   This section makes provision for the appointment to fee-paid judicial offices of those who have previously held corresponding salaried appointments. It adds two new sections, 94A and 94B, to the Constitutional Reform Act 2005. Subsections (1) and (2) of the new section 94A enable the Lord Chancellor to make appointments to fee-paid offices in the ordinary courts below the rank of circuit judge (and to fee-paid offices in courts established under armed forces legislation), without the JAC selection process applying. Such appointments may be made only with the concurrence of the Lord Chief Justice and provided the person holds a corresponding qualifying salaried office or has ceased to hold such an office within the two years immediately preceding the proposed appointment. Subsection (3) enables the Lord Chief Justice to delegate his power of concurrence. Section 94B makes corresponding provision to enable the Lord Chancellor to make such appointments in tribunals, covering the existing tribunals listed in Part 3 of Schedule 14 to the Constitutional Reform Act 2005 and the new tribunals created by Part 1 of this Act. These appointments require the concurrence of the Senior President of Tribunals. Where it is proposed to appoint a person as a deputy judge of the Upper Tribunal, and that person holds or held an office listed in section 6(1), the Lord Chancellor must also consult the Lord Chief Justice. The general 2-year limit is disapplied in relation to former judges of the High Court and above (and equivalents in Scotland and Northern Ireland) being appointed as deputy judges of the Upper Tribunal.

Section 54: Continuation of judicial office after normal retirement date

298.   Section 54 amends section 26 of the Judicial Pensions and Retirement Act 1993 to rectify a lacuna resulting from its modification by the Constitutional Reform Act 2005. Section 26 makes provision for the extension of service of judicial office holders beyond the retirement age otherwise prescribed by that Act. The modification made by the 2005 Act catered for the extension of service of judicial office holders exercising jurisdiction exclusively in one of the three legal jurisdictions of the United Kingdom but inadvertently omitted to cater for those exercising jurisdiction in two or all three of those legal jurisdictions. The new sub-sections of section 26 of the 1993 Act added by this section rectify the problem by conferring the power to extend service in such circumstances on the Senior President of Tribunals in respect of Tribunal offices listed in the new section 26 (12A) of the 1993 Act or otherwise by the Lord Chief Justice, in both cases subject to the concurrence of the Lord Chancellor.

Section 55: Appointment of deputy Circuit Judge

299.   Section 55 modifies section 24 of the Courts Act 1971 (as previously modified by the Constitutional Reform Act 2005) so that the responsibility for appointing as a deputy circuit judge someone who has previously held office as a judge of the Court

of Appeal or of the High Court, or as a circuit judge, is vested in the Lord Chancellor, with the concurrence of the Lord Chief Justice, rather than the other way round.

Section 56: Appointment of deputy district judges, etc

300.   Section 56 gives effect to Schedule 11.

Schedule 11: District judges and deputy district judges

301.   District judges and deputy district judges exercise jurisdiction, in England and Wales, in both the High Court and the county courts. For deputy district judges there are parallel appointment provisions in the Supreme Court Act 1981 (for deputy district judges in the High Court) and the County Courts Act 1984 (for deputy district judges in the county courts).

302.   Paragraph 2 enables the Lord Chief Justice to delegate to another judicial office holder his powers to assign district judges to one or more district registries of the High Court and his powers to change assignments. Paragraph 6 makes similar provision about the assignment of district judges to county court districts.

303.   Paragraph 3 amends the provisions in section 102 of the Supreme Court Act 1981 about the appointment of deputy district judges.

304.   Provision is made for appointments to be made by the Lord Chancellor, normally   subject to the Judicial Appointments Commission (JAC) selection process as prescribed under the Constitutional Reform Act 2005. A retirement age of 70 will apply to these post-holders (with the possibility of extension up to age 75).

305.   Further provision is made however that where a person holds or has previously within the last two years held the office of district judge, the Lord Chancellor may appoint that person as a deputy district judge, with the concurrence of the Lord Chief Justice, without that appointment being subject to selection by the JAC. Such persons may be appointed up to (but will have to retire by) the age of 75.

306.   The Lord Chief Justice is also given powers, after consulting the Lord Chancellor, to assign any deputy district judge to one or more district registries of the High Court, and to change the assignment. Deputy district judges are given powers to act in district registries to which they have not been assigned, but only in accordance with arrangements made by or on behalf of the Lord Chief Justice.

307.   Paragraph 4 makes transitional provision about existing deputy district judges: they continue to be deputy district judges, and are treated as having been assigned to the district registries for which they were appointed. In paragraph 4, the label "the commencement date" is given to the point in time at which paragraph 3 comes into force, not to the entire day at the beginning of which paragraph 3 comes into force.

308.   Paragraphs 7 and 10 make, for deputy district judges appointed under section 8 of the County Courts Act 1984, provision similar to that made by paragraphs 3 and 4. The paragraphs respectively modify the provisions in section 8 of the 1984 Act and make transitional provision.

309.   Paragraphs 8 and 9 make consequential amendments to the County Courts Act 1984. Paragraphs 11 to 13 make consequential amendments to the judicial-retirement provisions of the Judicial Pensions and Retirement Act 1993. Paragraphs 14 and 15 consequentially amend references to these appointments in other legislation.

Section 57: Deputy, and temporary additional, Masters etc.

310.   Section 57 amends the provisions in section 91 of the Supreme Court Act 1981 for appointing deputies and temporary officers to certain posts, including masters and registrars of the Supreme Court. Section 91 of the Supreme Court Act 1981 was amended by paragraph 139 of Schedule 4 to the Constitutional Reform Act 2005 to enable the Lord Chief Justice, after consulting the Lord Chancellor, to make appointments to these posts. Section 57 further amends the Supreme Court Act 1981, and the Constitutional Reform Act 2005, to provide that these appointments are now to be made by the Lord Chancellor, and will normally be subject to the JAC selection process under the 2005 Act. These appointments are added to Schedule 14 to the 2005 Act. However, provision is also made that where a person holds or has within the last two years held equivalent office on a salaried basis, the Lord Chancellor may with the concurrence of the Lord Chief Justice appoint him to a deputy or additional temporary office under section 91 of the Supreme Court Act 1981 without a JAC selection process. The section makes consequential amendments to the Supreme Court Act 1981, so that a retirement age of 75 will apply to those who have previously held salaried office. (The usual retirement age for appointments under section 91 is 70, with the possibility of annual extensions up to the age of 75.)

Section 58: Appointment of temporary assistant to Judge Advocate General

311.   The purpose of section 58 is to enable certain judicial office-holders and lawyers, who already have considerable experience of sitting as judge advocates in courts-martial, to continue to be eligible to sit as judge advocates once the Armed Forces Act 2006 is in force, without the need for selection by the Judicial Appointments Commission (JAC).

312.   A judge advocate is appointed by the Judge Advocate General to an individual court-martial. Under the current law, judge advocates must have a 5-year legal qualification, and the JAC is not involved in their selection.

313.   That position will change once section 362 of the Armed Forces Act 2006 (AFA) comes into force, which is expected to be in January 2009. The AFA defines Judges Advocates as (a) the Judge Advocate General (JAG); (b) a person appointed under section 30(1)(a) or (b) or (2) of the Court-Martial (Appeals) Act 1951 ("the 1951 Act") (Vice JAG, Assistant JAG, and temporary assistants to JAG); or (c) a puisne judge of the High Court of England and Wales who, following advice from the Judge Advocate General, is nominated by or on behalf of the Lord Chief Justice of England and Wales to sit as a Judge Advocate.

314.   Once implemented this provision will mean that, apart from High Court judges and the Judge Advocate General himself, only persons appointed under s. 30 of the 1951 Act may be appointed as judge advocates. However, appointments under s. 30 of the 1951 Act require a selection by the JAC.

315.   Over the past few years, the Judge Advocate General has adopted the practice of appointing judge advocates both from persons holding salaried office under s. 30 of the 1951 Act (ie Vice JAG and Assistant JAG), and also from a pool of qualified lawyers and judicial office holders, which currently numbers 12 individuals. The purpose of these amendments is to enable this pool to carry on sitting as judge advocates once the AFA is in force, without the need for a JAC competition. This section will amend the 1951 Act so that no JAC selection will be required for

appointments to the position of temporary assistant to the Judge Advocate General under s.30(2) of the 1951 Act where the appointee has, within the last two years, been appointed as a judge advocate to a court-martial by the Judge Advocate General. However, the concurrence of the Lord Chief Justice is required for such appointments. Once a person has been appointed to the position of temporary assistant to the Judge Advocate General, he will be eligible to sit as judge advocate in a Court Martial when the Armed Forces Act 2006 is in force. This section will enable the pool of 12 judicial office-holders or lawyers, from which appointments as judge advocates are currently made, to continue sitting as judge advocates.

Section 59: Members and chairmen of certain Appeals Commissions

316.   Section 59 amends Part 3 of Schedule 14 to the Constitutional Reform Act 2005 to remove references to the offices of member, and Chairman, of: the Special Immigration Appeals Commission; the Proscribed Organisations Appeal Commission; and the Pathogens Access Appeal Commission. Candidates for these appointments will no longer be required to go through the Judicial Appointments Commission selection process. In practice, the legally qualified members and the Chairmen of these Commissions are appointed only from among serving senior judges. Once section 59 is in force, appointments will continue to be made by the Lord Chancellor, but it is intended that he will seek nominations for these posts from the Lord Chief Justice. If the Lord Chancellor wishes to be given assistance in making appointments to these Commissions, it will be possible for him to ask for assistance from the Judicial Appointments Commission under section 98 of the Constitutional Reform Act 2005.

Section 60: Appointment as Chairman of Law Commission

317.   This section makes provision for the Lord Chancellor to select the Chairman of the Law Commission from serving members of the senior judiciary only, by making changes to section 1 of the Law Commissions Act 1965 (c.22). The 'senior judiciary' for these purposes are the judges of the High Court and the judges of the Court of Appeal in England and Wales. This change reflects what has happened in practice since the establishment of the Law Commission.

Section 61: Orders permitting disclosures to Judicial Appointments Commission

318.   Section 5A of the Justice (Northern Ireland) Act 2002 ('the 2002 Act') confers power to disclose information to the Northern Ireland Judicial Appointments Commission for the purposes of selection for appointment to judicial office in Northern Ireland. Section 5A(1) of the 2002 Act provides that information held by 'permitted persons' may be disclosed to the Commission for the purposes of making any such selection. Section 5A(5) of that Act specifies a number of 'permitted persons' for the purpose of section 5A. Section 5A(6), which has yet to be commenced, provides that the Lord Chancellor may by order designate other persons, who exercise functions which he considers are of a public nature, as 'permitted persons'. The order-making power contained in section 5A(6) is not, however, currently subject to any Parliamentary control. Section 61 remedies this anomaly by subjecting the order-making power contained in section 5A(6) to the negative resolution procedure.

PART 3: ENFORCEMENT BY TAKING CONTROL OF GOODS

SUMMARY

319.　　Part 3 of the Act unifies the law governing the activities of enforcement agents when taking control of and selling goods, and requires such agents (with certain exceptions) to hold a valid certificate issued by a county court. It also modernises and unifies most of the terminology used in various pieces of legislation where the new unified procedure will apply.

320.　　Part 3 also abolishes the common law right to distrain for rent arrears and replaces it with a new, more limited right and a modified 'out of court' regime for recovering rent arrears due under a lease of commercial premises.

BACKGROUND

Procedure

321.　　At present the law relating to enforcement by the seizure and sale of goods is complex and can be unclear and confusing. It is contained in numerous statutes, secondary legislation and common law and its language is old fashioned. There are various terms that describe this enforcement process, for example execution, distress and levy and various different procedures depending on the type of debt which is being recovered. *Effective Enforcement* recommended the terminology should be modernised and the procedure reformed.

322.　　*Effective Enforcement* also identified that persons who currently take control of goods are not subject to any uniform regulatory system and highlighted anecdotal evidence of some enforcement agents threatening and intimidating vulnerable debtors. *Effective Enforcement* therefore proposed a system to guard against malpractice and to protect debtors. It is intended (in the longer term) that a licensing regime will be put in place, implemented via a regulatory body. While this is being taken forward independently, as detailed below, as an interim measure the Act replaces (and extends and modifies) the certification process that currently exists for bailiffs under the Law of Distress Amendment Act 1888. The extended and modified certification process will apply to persons taking control of goods who are not Crown employees or constables (the justification for such an exclusion being that Crown employees and constables, by virtue of their status, are already subject to adequate systems of control). A consultative Partial Regulatory Impact Assessment was issued on 30 January 2007 exploring the costs and impact of a licensing regime via a regulatory body. This sets out the options for the future regulation of enforcement agents who are not Crown employees.

Rent Arrears Recovery

323.　　Distress for rent is a summary remedy which enables landlords to recover rent arrears without going to court, by taking goods from the let premises and either holding them until the arrears are paid or selling them. It is an ancient common law remedy which, over time, has been extended and modified by successive statutes.

324.　　The Law Commission's Report concluded that distress for rent has a number of features which make it inherently unjust to tenants, to third parties and to other creditors and recommended its abolition.

325.   Following a period of consultation, the Government decided to accept the Law Commission's recommendation. However, the consultation revealed that distress for rent is an effective remedy for recovering rent arrears, particularly for commercial properties. If it were to be abolished without any replacement, the Government concluded that there could be disadvantages both to landlords and to tenants of commercial properties.

326.   The Act therefore abolishes the current law on distress for rent and replaces it with a modified regime (called Commercial Rent Arrears Recovery or CRAR) for recovering rent arrears due under leases of commercial premises.

COMMENTARY ON SECTIONS: PART 3

Section 62: Enforcement by taking control of goods

327.   This section gives effect to Schedules 12 and 13 to the Act. Certain current powers to seize and sell goods can only be exercised according to the procedure for taking control of and selling goods detailed in Schedule 12.

328.   The terminology in the various pieces of primary legislation relating to these powers has been amended, and some of the warrants and writs which give these powers, namely warrants of execution, warrants of distress and writs of fieri facias (except writs of fieri facias de bonis ecclesiasticis), are renamed warrants of control and writs of control.

329.   A warrant of execution empowers a district judge to seize and sell a debtor's goods for the purpose of recovering money payable under a county court judgment or order. A warrant of distress may be issued by a magistrates' court for the purpose of recovering a sum adjudged to be paid by a conviction or order of the court. The warrant requires the sum to be recovered by seizure and sale of the debtor's goods. A writ of fieri facias requires a sheriff or enforcement officer to seize and sell a debtor's goods for the purpose of recovering a sum due under a High Court judgment or order. A writ of fieri facias de bonis ecclesiasticis requires the bishop to seize a debtor's ecclesiastical property in order to satisfy a High Court judgment. As writs of fieri facias de bonis ecclesiasticis are unique and because of the special role of the bishop, they are not renamed (nor are they subject to the new unified procedure detailed in Schedule 12).

330.   A writ or warrant of delivery is a writ/warrant to enforce an order for the delivery of particular goods that are identified in the writ/warrant. A writ or warrant of possession is a writ/warrant issued to enforce an order for possession of land.

331.   Schedule 13 makes amendments to existing primary legislation, which are necessary to give effect to these changes or as a result of them.

Schedule 12: Taking control of goods

332.   This Schedule prescribes a new procedure to be followed by enforcement agents when seizing and selling goods pursuant to powers under High Court writs of execution, county court warrants of execution, certain magistrates' court warrants of distress, High Court writs and county court warrants of delivery and possession which contain a power to seize and sell goods and the following enactments as amended by Schedule 13:

- Sections 4 and 16 of the Inclosure Act 1773;

- Section 91 of the Lands Clauses Consolidation Act 1845;

- Sections 151 and 159 of the Inclosure Act 1845;

- Section 33 of the Railways Clauses Act 1863;

- Section 13 of the Compulsory Purchase Act 1965;

- Section 61 of the Taxes Management Act 1970;

- Section 76 of the Magistrates' Court Act 1980;

- Section 85 of the County Courts Act 1984;

- Section 62A of the Local Government Finance Act 1988;

- Section 35 of the Child Support Act 1991;

- Schedule 15, paragraph 12 of the Water Resources Act 1991;

- Section 54 of the Land Drainage Act 1991;

- Section 121A of the Social Security Administration Act 1992;

- Section 14 of the Local Government Finance Act 1992;

- Section 51 of the Finance Act 1997;

- Schedule 12, paragraph 1A of the Finance Act 2003;

- Section 72 of the Tribunals, Courts and Enforcement Act 2007.

333.   The Schedule prescribes, or enables regulations to prescribe, the entire process to be followed by enforcement agents when taking control of and selling goods under the above mentioned powers, from the serving of a notice, to taking control of goods (including which goods may be taken), powers of entry, goods which may be seized, care of goods seized, the sale of goods seized and the distribution of the sale proceeds.

334.   On the issue of which goods may be taken, the Schedule provides that all goods of the debtor may be seized other than those which are exempt (as prescribed in regulations) or protected under any other enactment. Examples of protection from seizure are:

- any statutory state or diplomatic immunity;

- personal property of a trustee pursuant to section 23 of the Trade Union and Labour Relations (Consolidation) Act 1992;

- works of art from abroad loaned for temporary exhibitions and protected under section 135 of the Tribunals, Courts and Enforcement Act 2007.

335.   The Schedule also enables regulations to specify fees, charges and expenses that can be charged by a person in connection with taking control of goods (by way of example, the fees charged by an enforcement agent for taking control of goods). Such regulations will specify when and how such fees, charges and expenses will be recoverable from the debtor, to include when such amounts can be deducted from the proceeds of sale of any goods. The regulations may also specify that any disputed amount of such fees, costs and expenses is to be assessed in accordance with rules of court.

336.   In addition, the Schedule sets out the remedial action and the level of damages available to a debtor against an enforcement agent who breaches the procedure. The Schedule does not make any provision for the debtor's right to bring a claim against an enforcement agent whose actions were not authorised at the outset because this is already covered by the existing law of tort. The Schedule also specifies the circumstances when a creditor can bring a claim against the debtor and it creates offences of intentionally obstructing an enforcement agent in the lawful exercise of his power and interfering with goods seized.

Schedule 13: Taking control of goods: amendments

337.   This Schedule amends the existing legislation referred to in paragraph 332 under which the unified procedure in Schedule 12 will be used. It also contains amendments consequential on the introduction of the new procedure and terminology. So, where appropriate, references to warrants of execution and warrants of distress are amended to warrants of control, references to writs of fieri facias are amended to writs of control, references to distrain and distraint are amended to taking control of goods and references to walking possession agreements are amended to controlled goods agreements.

338.   A walking possession agreement is an agreement between the person who has the power to seize the goods ("the distrainor") and the debtor. The distrainor agrees that the debtor can retain possession of the goods without anyone being left on the premises to guard them. In return, the debtor agrees not to remove the goods until he makes payment for the debt and that the distrainor may return to the premises at a later date to remove the goods for sale if payment is not made.

339.   In addition, where a power to distrain is not currently set out on the face of an Act, but instead secondary legislation under the Act authorises distraint, the Schedule amends the Act so that the power to distrain (which becomes a power to use the procedure in Schedule 12) is on the face of the Act rather than in secondary legislation.

Section 63: Enforcement agents

340.   This section specifies the criteria to be met for an individual to act as an enforcement agent. This includes acting under a certificate under section 64. The section also creates an offence where an individual acts as an enforcement agent and does not meet any of the specified criteria.

Section 64: Certificates to act as an enforcement agent

341.   This section specifies who may issue a certificate under which an enforcement agent can act. The section also provides that the Lord Chancellor must make provision about certificates by regulations. The provision may include, for example, conditions that may apply to issued certificates, provision about the suspension and cancellation of certificates, and provision for reasonable fees to be charged for applications for certificates.

342.   Subsection (4) enables enforcement agents who currently hold a certificate issued under section 7 of the Law of Distress Amendment Act 1888 to continue to operate under that certificate. After the certificate expires, regulations will specify that a certificate will need to be issued in accordance with the new certification provisions under this section.

Section 65: Common law rules replaced

343.   This section provides for the replacement of the common law rules about how the powers to take control of and sell goods are exercised. The provisions in Chapter 1, in particular Schedule 12, replace these common law rules. The replacement of the common law rules includes those that relate to remedies that are currently available to debtors (including replevin) and offences by debtors (such as rescuing goods seized). Replevin is a process by which the owner can recover goods seized in return for an undertaking to bring proceedings to determine the right to seize the goods and for tendering sufficient security for the debt and the proceedings. Rescuing goods is where a person interferes with goods seized.

344.   Under section 66 these common law rules will continue to apply in relation to those goods that have been distrained before the new procedure comes into force.

Section 66: Pre-commencement enforcement not affected

345.   This section provides that the new procedure for taking control of and selling goods does not affect any power to distrain where the goods were distrained against or made subject to a walking possession agreement before the new procedure comes into force.

Section 67: Transfer of county court enforcement

346.   This section transfers the district judge's responsibility for the execution of warrants of control issued by a county court to any person authorised by or on behalf of the Lord Chancellor. (Section 85(2) of the County Courts Act 1984 refers to the "registrar" but, by virtue of section 74 of the Courts and Legal Services Act 1990, the office of "registrar" is now abolished and replaced by "district judge".) In practice, the warrants will be executed by county court bailiffs (who will continue to be known as county court bailiffs).

Section 68: Magistrates' courts warrants of control

347.   This section creates a new section 125ZA of the Magistrates' Courts Act 1980 so as to provide for the endorsement of warrants of control issued by the magistrates' court in line with the endorsement process for High Court writs under Schedule 7 to the Courts Act 2003 (and in line with section 69 on county court warrants). The new section is referred to in paragraph 4 of Schedule 12.

Section 69: County court warrants of control etc

348.   This section replaces the existing section 99 of the County Courts Act 1984. It applies to warrants of control issued by a county court and warrants of delivery and warrants of possession which include a power to take control of goods and sell them. It details the procedure for endorsing county court warrants in line with High Court writs. The order of priority in execution is dictated by the date and time of endorsement. The new section is referred to in paragraph 4 of Schedule 12.

Section 70: Power of High Court to stay execution

349.   This section gives the High Court the power to stay execution of a writ of control for such period of time and on such conditions as the court determines in line with the county court's power to stay execution. The power may only be exercised where the court is satisfied that the debtor is unable to pay any sum or instalment of any sum recovered against him.

Section 71: Abolition of common law right

350.   This section abolishes the common law right to distrain for arrears of rent. Statutory repeals are dealt with in Schedule 14 and Part 4 of Schedule 22. Taken together, these provisions will sweep away the existing law on distress for rent.

351.   Distress for rent is a summary remedy which enables landlords to recover rent arrears, without going to court, by taking goods from the demised premises and either holding them until the arrears are paid or selling them. At common law, the right of distress for rent arises automatically by virtue of the landlord and tenant relationship. So the remedy is almost always available to the landlord of premises, whether residential or commercial premises, when rent is in arrears. Distress for rent is an ancient common law remedy which, over time, has been extended and modified by statute.

352.   The right to distrain has applied to different kinds of rent, including rentcharges. This section and the statutory repeals will abolish distress for all forms of rent (see, for example, the repeal of section 121(1) of the Law of Property Act 1925, which confers statutory power to distrain for a rentcharge).

Section 72: Commercial rent arrears recovery (CRAR)

353.   This section creates a new statutory right for a landlord of commercial premises to recover rent arrears by using the procedure in Schedule 12 for taking control of the tenant's goods. This allows the landlord to enter the let premises in order to take goods belonging to the tenant, then sell those goods and recover the rent arrears from the proceeds of sale. The right, which is called CRAR (commercial rent arrears recovery), replaces the existing right of distress for rent. But in contrast to distress, CRAR is available only to landlords of commercial premises.

Section 73: Landlord

354.   This section defines "landlord" for the purposes of CRAR and accordingly identifies the person to whom CRAR is available. The definition in this section reflects the position in the current law of distress for rent as to who can distrain for rent arrears.

355.   Subsection (1) sets out the general rule that the landlord is the person entitled to the immediate reversion in the property comprised in the lease. This is the person to whom the property will revert at the end of the lease.

356.   In most cases it will be clear who is entitled to the immediate reversion of the property. However, subsections (3) to (7) clarify the position in four particular circumstances, each reflecting the current law on distress for rent. The circumstances are:

- (in subsection (3)) where the premises are let under a tenancy by estoppel;
- (in subsection (4)) where the premises are let by joint landlords;
- (in subsection (5) and (6)) where the let premises have been mortgaged;
- (in subsection (7)) where the court has appointed a receiver to deal with the let premises.

357.   In the case of a tenancy by estoppel, the landlord may not have a legal estate in the land comprised in the lease, in which case he will not be entitled to the

immediate reversion in that property. Subsection (3) makes it clear that such a person will nevertheless be a "landlord" for the purposes of CRAR and may therefore use CRAR to recover rent arrears from his tenant, provided that all the other conditions are satisfied.

358.   Subsection (4) provides that if the premises are let under a joint tenancy, then any one of the persons who hold the legal estate will be the "landlord" for the purposes of CRAR. This means that any one of them may exercise CRAR and may do so to recover the rent due to all of them.

359.   Subsections (5) and (6) deal with mortgaged properties. If the premises are let by a person who has taken out a mortgage on the property, then that person (who is the "mortgagor" or borrower) will normally be the "landlord" who is entitled to use CRAR to recover rent due under that lease. But if, at any time, the mortgagee (the lender) gives notice of his intention to repossess the property, then he will become the landlord thereafter in relation to that existing lease.

360.   However, as with the current law on distress for rent, a mortgagee who becomes the landlord in this way will not be able to use CRAR to recover rent due under the existing lease if that lease is not binding on the mortgagee. This is because there will be no relationship of landlord and tenant between the mortgagee and the tenant under the existing lease. A lease will not be binding on the mortgagee if it is made after the mortgage was created, and if it is not made under either:

- an express leasing power contained in the mortgage deed, or

- section 99 of the Law of the Property Act 1925 (leasing powers of mortgagor and mortgagee in possession).

361.   By virtue of subsection (7), a receiver who has been appointed by the court in relation to the property that is subject to the lease may exercise CRAR in the name of the landlord.

362.   Subsection (8) provides that a landlord who has a right to use CRAR will need to authorise a certificated enforcement agent to exercise CRAR on his behalf (unless he himself is a certificated enforcement agent; see paragraph 2 of Schedule 12). The landlord will need to instruct the enforcement agent in writing. The form, content, and other requirements in relation to the written instructions from the landlord to the enforcement agent will be prescribed by way of secondary legislation.

363.   Subsection (9) provides that any person who has a statutory right under any other legislation to use CRAR, is to be treated as "the landlord" for the purposes of CRAR.

Section 74: Lease

364.   This section defines the term "lease". A lease means any lease that may exist in law or in equity. This section makes it clear that a "lease" includes a tenancy at will, but does not include a tenancy at sufferance. So, for the purposes of CRAR, a "lease" includes all forms of lease, including long leases, short tenancies, tenancies by estoppel and other equitable leases.

365.   A lease must, however, be evidenced in writing. The intention is to ensure that CRAR can only be used in circumstances where the main terms of the lease (particularly the rent) are clear and certain to the parties concerned.

Section 75: Commercial premises

366.   This section defines what is meant by "a lease of commercial premises". A lease (lease A) will not be "a lease of commercial premises" if any part of the let premises is let under lease A (or let under any sublease B) as a dwelling, or occupied as a dwelling. So, for example, a lease of property comprising a shop and a flat will not be a lease of commercial premises if the flat is used, or is required by the lease to be used, as a dwelling. But if that lease does not impose any requirements as to the use of the flat, and the tenant chooses to use it either as a storeroom or office for the shop, then the lease will be one of commercial premises because no part of the demised premises is let or occupied as a dwelling.

367.   This section makes it clear that any occupation as a dwelling will not count if it is in breach of the terms of lease A or any lease that is superior to lease A. Similarly if the property has been sublet then any sub-letting as a dwelling will not count if it is in breach of the terms of a lease that is superior to lease B. The purpose of these provisions is to ensure that a commercial tenant cannot seek to prevent his landlord from using CRAR against him by, for example, allowing a third party to occupy part of the premises as a dwelling. So the landlord can still use CRAR against his tenant in those circumstances, even though there are residential occupiers present. But the provisions are also designed to ensure that a landlord (who is himself a commercial tenant under lease A) cannot rely on his own breach of lease A to use CRAR against the tenants to whom he has sublet the property as a dwelling under lease B. So in those circumstances, the landlord cannot use CRAR because lease B will not be a lease of commercial premises.

Section 76: Rent

368.   This section defines rent for the purposes of its recovery by CRAR, as the sum payable by the tenant for the possession and use of the premises under the lease, including any interest payable on that sum and any VAT chargeable on the sum or the interest.

369.   Any amounts not directly attributable to the tenant's possession and use of the premises do not qualify e.g. council tax. This is the case even if the lease defines them as rent.

370.   The rent may be merged with other sums so that it is payable as a combined figure, the individual figure not being known or able to be ascertained. In this situation, the rent will be considered to be that portion of the total sum as reasonably reflects the amount payable for the possession and use of the premises.

371.   Rent which is payable under or by virtue of Part 2 of the Landlord and Tenant Act 1954 (c. 56) is deemed to be rent as defined by the section, and is therefore recoverable by CRAR. Part 2 of the 1954 Act gives security of tenure to business leases, so that they are not ended by the expiry of the contractual term, but continue until terminated in accordance with the provisions of Part 2.

372.   The definition of rent given by this section, however, is not congruent with the meaning of rent at section 71 (abolition of common law right) because section 71 relates to a wider range of rents for which the right to the old remedy of distress for rent exists. For that reason, the interpretation of "rent" in this section does not apply to section 71 (see section 87). The definition also does not apply to section 85 which defines "rent" for its own purposes.

Section 77: The rent recoverable

373.   This section sets out the conditions that must be met for the right to CRAR to become exercisable. The conditions are:

- the tenant is in arrears of rent before notice of enforcement is given;

- the amount of the arrears owed by the tenant is certain, or capable of being calculated with certainty; and

- the "net unpaid rent" equals or exceeds a set amount to be prescribed in regulations.

374.   The requirement that the net unpaid rent must equal or exceed the prescribed minimum is a condition that must be satisfied at two stages: first, before the landlord gives notice of enforcement and, second, before he takes control of goods under Schedule 12. This means that the landlord will need to recalculate the "net unpaid rent" immediately before he takes control of goods. If the recalculated figure is lower than the prescribed minimum, it will not be permissible for the landlord to proceed to take control of goods.

375.   The "net unpaid rent" is the amount of unpaid rent less any interest or VAT that may be payable on that amount and less any "permitted deductions". Permitted deductions from rent are deductions that a tenant is presently entitled to make from his rent under statute, at common law and in equity. Examples include sums that may be deducted or recouped from, or set off against, rent:

- under the terms of the lease;

- in respect of damages for the landlord's breach of his obligations to repair (or the cost of repairs, if carried out at the tenant's expense);

- in respect of damages for the landlord's breach of the covenant of quiet enjoyment;

- in respect of statutory compensation for improvements under section 11(2) of the Landlord and Tenant Act 1954.

376.   The amount of rent that a landlord is entitled to recover by CRAR is the amount of unpaid rent less any permitted deductions that the tenant is entitled to make against that rent.

Section 78: Intervention of the court

377.   This section sets out the powers of the High Court or a county court, as rules of court may provide, to intervene in the exercise of CRAR. The court's power arises only where the following conditions are met: firstly, notice of enforcement has been served on the tenant; secondly, the tenant has made an application to the court to intervene; and thirdly, the court is satisfied that the circumstances meet the prescribed grounds for intervening.

378.   The court then has two options available to it. It may make an order to set aside the notice of enforcement, which effectively cancels that notice and prevents the landlord from taking any further steps under CRAR in relation to that notice. This would occur, for example, if the court considered that the preconditions for exercising CRAR had not been met.

379.   Alternatively, the court may suspend the use of CRAR, by making an order that no further steps may be taken in exercise of CRAR without further order by the court. This might occur, for example, if there is a genuine dispute about the amount of rent in arrears or the calculation of the net unpaid rent. In those circumstances, the court may suspend the use of CRAR until that dispute is resolved.

Section 79: Use of CRAR after end of lease

380.   This section deals with the use of CRAR after a lease has ended. The provisions of this section are intended broadly to reflect the current law governing the availability of distress for rent after a lease has ended. Subsection (1) sets out the general rule that, when the lease ends, CRAR will cease to be available. But that is subject to two exceptions.

381.   The first exception is set out in subsection (2). This ensures that a landlord who has taken control of goods under CRAR before the lease comes to an end (or under the second exception, below), is not prevented from completing the process by selling those goods.

382.   The second exception is set out in subsections (3) and (4) and this is intended to preserve the effect of sections 6 and 7 of the Landlord and Tenant Act 1709 after those provisions are repealed by this Act (see Schedule 14). This exception applies where the tenant remains in occupation after the lease comes to an end. It allows the landlord to use CRAR for no more than six months after the lease has come to an end, provided that the lease was not ended by forfeiture, the landlord and tenant remain the same and, if a new lease has been granted to the tenant, it must be a lease of commercial premises. For this purpose it does not matter whether the new lease of commercial premises is in writing or not because the section only permits the landlord to recover rent due under the expired lease of commercial premises, which must be in writing.

383.   Subsection (7) defines when a lease ends for the purposes of this section.

Section 80: Agricultural holdings

384.   This section makes a couple of special provisions in relation to the exercise of CRAR where the let premises is an agricultural holding. It is intended to preserve the effect of sections 16 and 17 of the Agricultural Holdings Act 1986 for the purposes of CRAR. (Sections 16 to 19 of that Act will be repealed by this Act; see Schedule 14).

385.   First, there is a limitation on the rent that can be recovered by a landlord of an agricultural holding because CRAR cannot be used to recover rent that became due more than one year before the notice of enforcement is given. Second, any compensation that is due to the tenant under the Agricultural Holdings Act 1986 will be a "permitted deduction" for the purposes of CRAR, provided that the amount of compensation has been ascertained (for the meaning of "permitted deductions", see section 77(7)).

Section 81: Right to rent from sub-tenant

386.   This section makes provision for a landlord who is entitled to use CRAR against his immediate tenant to instead serve a notice on any sub-tenant requiring that sub-tenant to pay his rent directly to him, instead of paying it to his own landlord in the usual way. Its purpose is to allow the landlord to recover, from a sub-tenant, arrears of rent that are due to him from the immediate tenant.

387.   The section is intended to preserve the effect of sections 3 and 6 of the Law of Distress Amendment Act 1908 (which will be repealed by this Act, see Schedule 14) in a form that is consistent with the other provisions of CRAR.

388.   Where a notice is given to a sub-tenant under this section, it must set out the amount of the arrears owed to the landlord (the superior landlord) by the immediate tenant. The notice must also require the sub-tenant to pay his rent directly to the superior landlord instead of paying it to his own landlord, until the amount of arrears specified in the notice have been paid off, or rent ceases to be payable by the sub-tenant (for example, if he moves on), or the notice is replaced or withdrawn by the superior landlord.

389.   Subsection (5) enables regulations to determine when a notice given by the landlord on a sub-tenant under this section takes effect.

390.   For as long as the notice has effect, the superior landlord will effectively stand in place of the sub-tenant's landlord for the purpose of recovering, receiving or discharging any rent payable by the sub-tenant under the notice, but only for that purpose. This means that the superior landlord can recover from the sub-tenant the amount stated in the notice by using CRAR. But the superior landlord cannot recover that sum from the sub-tenant by serving another section 81 notice on an inferior sub-tenant (see section 84).

391.   The superior landlord may serve more than one notice under this section, but any later notice replaces an earlier one and where the landlord serves a later notice on a different sub-tenant he must withdraw the earlier one (see section 83). This ensures that only one notice has effect at any one time.

Section 82: Off-setting payments under a notice

392.   This section applies where a landlord has given notice to a sub-tenant under section 81.

393.   Any sums that the sub-tenant pays under the notice to the superior landlord will be deductible from the amount of rent he would otherwise have had to pay to his own landlord. So, if the sub-tenant is required to pay £250 a month to the superior landlord under a notice (i.e., until the stated arrears are paid off), then he is entitled to deduct £250 a month from his own rent for as long as he is required to continue making payments under that notice. If there is a hierarchy of sub-leases and the landlord serves notice on an inferior sub-tenant, then this diversion of rent may be passed up the hierarchy of superior sub-tenants until ultimately it is deducted from rent payable to the (defaulting) immediate tenant. For example, where the notice is served on sub- tenant C, he may deduct any sums paid to the superior landlord from rent due to his own landlord (sub-tenant B). Sub-tenant B may then deduct an equivalent amount from his landlord (sub-tenant A) and sub-tenant A may deduct an equivalent amount from his landlord (the immediate tenant).

394.   Payments under a section 81 notice will continue to be deductible from rent in this way, even after the arrears stated in the notice have been paid or the notice has been replaced by one served on another sub-tenant, unless the sub-tenant is aware of those facts. So a payment under a section 81 notice will not be deductible from rent if, at the time it is made:

  • the landlord has already withdrawn the notice;

- the paying sub-tenant has already made payments under the notice that total an amount at least equal to the arrears stated in that notice;

- the paying sub-tenant knows that the arrears stated in the notice have already been paid off by some other means (e.g., by the immediate tenant).

395.   Similarly, part of a payment under a section 81 notice will not be deductible from rent if, at the time it was made, that part of the payment, when added together with earlier payments made by the sub-tenant, at least equal the arrears stated in the notice.

Section 83: Withdrawal and replacement of notices

396.   If a landlord gives a section 81 notice to a sub-tenant, but subsequently gives another section 81 notice to the same or another sub-tenant for the same amount of arrears (or an amount including all or part of it) then the later notice will automatically replace the earlier notice. This ensures that, for any amount of arrears, there is no more than one notice in force at any one time. (There is an exception to this rule as explained in the next paragraph).

397.   There may be cases where, for instance, a landlord (A) lets premises to tenant (B) and tenant (B) geographically divides the premises by letting, say, the ground floor to sub-tenant (C) and the first floor to sub-tenant (D). The rent owed to B in respect of the premises is, therefore, shared between C and D. Under the provisions of this section, were B to default on rent owed to A, A will be able to serve notices on both C and D since they are not inferior or superior to one another (see subsection 83(2)(b)) in the hierarchy of tenancies. However, in the scenario described above, if C and D were superior or inferior to one another in the hierarchy of sub-tenancies, A would have to decide whether to serve a notice either on C or on D but not on both of them.

398.   A section 81 notice will cease to have effect when the amount of arrears stated in the notice has been paid off, or when the notice is replaced by a subsequent notice (see section 81). A paying sub-tenant will always know that a section 81 notice has ceased to have effect when he himself pays an amount equal to the stated amount of arrears. But he may not necessarily know, for example, that the immediate tenant has paid off the arrears, or that the landlord has served a replacement notice on another sub-tenant. For that reason, this section requires the landlord to withdraw a section 81 notice when that notice is replaced by another one, and when the amount in arrears is paid (unless it is paid wholly by the paying sub-tenant). This will ensure that the paying sub-tenant is fully informed about the status of the notice that has been given to him.

Section 84: Recovery of sums due and overpayments

399.   Subsections (1) and (2) deal with the recovery of sums due from a sub-tenant under a section 81 notice. If a notice has been given to a sub-tenant, but that sub-tenant fails to pay the amount of arrears stated in the notice, then the superior landlord can recover that amount from him and he may use CRAR to do so. But the superior landlord cannot recover that sum from the paying sub-tenant by giving another section 81 notice to an inferior sub-tenant (see section 84).

400.   Subsections (3) and (4) deal with overpayments to the superior landlord under a section 81 notice which has ceased to have effect, for example, because the stated

amount of arrears have been paid off or the landlord has given a replacement notice. These provisions ensure that any amount paid to the superior landlord under a section 81 notice will always count as if it were rent paid by the defaulting tenant (the immediate tenant). So any payment towards the stated amount of arrears will reduce those arrears and any overpayment (i.e. in excess of the stated amount of arrears) will constitute a credit against future rent due from the immediate tenant. If the immediate tenant has moved on, such that no future rent is due from him, then any overpayment under the notice will be treated as if it had been paid by him by mistake so that he may recover that payment from the superior landlord. But this does not affect any claim that the paying sub-tenant may have under the general law to recover or set-off the amount that he overpaid.

Section 85: Contracts for similar rights to be void

401.   This section ensures that any contractual provision which gives a landlord a power to recover rent (or other similar types of payment) by taking control of, or selling, goods or which modifies a landlord's right to commercial rent arrears recovery (CRAR), will be void, i.e., have no legal effect. A contractual provision that seeks to do any of these things will accordingly be unenforceable. But contracts will be valid and enforceable to the extent that they prevent or restrict the use of CRAR. For example, a contract may provide that:

- the landlord may not use CRAR to recover arrears of rent under the lease, whether during a particular period or at all; or

- he may use CRAR, but if he does so he may not take control of certain goods (which he would otherwise be entitled to take control of under paragraphs 3(1) and 9 of Schedule 12).

402.   This section is accordingly intended to prevent a landlord from making contracts to enlarge his power to take control of goods by CRAR or side-step the abolition of rent distress. For example, it will prevent a landlord from including any of the following provisions in a contract:

- a provision that gives a power to distrain for rent arrears, e.g., in relation to a lease of residential premises;

- a provision that extends the right to use CRAR, e.g. in relation to payments that are not 'rent' for the purposes of CRAR;

- a provision that modifies the procedures applying to CRAR, e.g. by dispensing with the need to give an enforcement notice.

Section 86: Amendments

403.   This section introduces the minor and consequential amendments relating to this Chapter that are contained in Schedule 14. These include amendments to abolish statutory powers to distrain for rentcharges (conferred by, for example, section 121(2) of the Law of Property Act 1925).

404.   It is not considered necessary to make any amendment to the Lodgers' Goods Protection Act 1871. Although there has been some doubt as to the extent of its repeal under section 8 of the Law of Distress Amendment 1908, it is considered that the Act is now wholly repealed by virtue of that enactment and section 132 of, and Schedule 6 to, the Judgements (Enforcement) Act (Northern Ireland) 1969. In any event, if not

wholly repealed, the Lodgers' Goods Protection Act 1871 would now be superseded by the abolition of the common law to distrain for rent arrears under section 71.

Section 88: Abolition of Crown preference

405.   This section abolishes the rule that distraint for debts owed to the Crown takes priority over enforcement of other debts by seizure and sale of goods. This builds upon previous similar changes abolishing priority being given to debts owed to the Crown above other debts in matters of bankruptcy and insolvency.

Section 89: Application to the Crown

406.   This section provides that Part 3 of the Act applies to the Crown (so that the Crown is able to recover debts due to it by using the new procedure under Part 3, and may not use the old law of distress where Part 3 abolishes it) but that the enforcement powers created by Part 3 cannot be used to recover debts due from the Crown, to take control of or sell Crown goods or to enter premises which the Crown occupies.

Section 90: Regulations

407.   This section contains definitions for "prescribed" and "regulations", under which powers to make regulations under Part 3 are exercisable by the Lord Chancellor. It sets out the parliamentary scrutiny applying to regulations under this Part, and provides for the power to make regulations to include power to make supplementary, consequential or transitional provision. Parliamentary scrutiny will be by way of the negative resolution procedure, other than for those powers contained at paragraphs 24(2) and 31(5) of Schedule 12, which will be by way of the affirmative resolution procedure.

PART 4: ENFORCEMENT OF JUDGMENTS AND ORDERS

SUMMARY

408.   Part 4 of the Act makes a number of changes to existing court-based methods of enforcing debts in the civil courts. Part 4 also contains new provisions, including powers to obtain information about debtors.

BACKGROUND

Attachment of earnings orders

409.   An attachment of earnings order (AEO) is a means of securing payment of certain debts by requiring an employer to make deductions direct from an employed debtor's earnings. Currently, the rate of deductions under an AEO made to secure payment of a judgment debt is calculated by a county court using information provided by the debtor.

410.   *Effective Enforcement* identified weaknesses in the current system and in particular the fact that information provided by debtors is often unreliable. The Act tackles this by making provision for a new method of calculation of deductions from earnings based on fixed rates, similar to the system used for council tax AEOs. Another weakness of the AEO system is that if a debtor changes job and does not inform the court of his new employer's details, the AEO lapses. The Act therefore enables the High Court, county courts, magistrates' courts and fines officers to request the name and address of the debtor's new employer from Her Majesty's Revenue and Customs ("HMRC"), for the purpose of redirecting the AEO.

Charging orders

411.   A charging order is a means of securing payment of a sum of money ordered to be paid under a judgment or order of the High Court or a county court by placing a charge onto the debtor's property (usually a house or land or securities such as shares). A charging order can be made absolute or subject to conditions. Once an order is in place, a creditor can subsequently apply to court seeking an order for sale of the charged property.

412.   At present, the court cannot make a charging order when payments due under an instalment order made to secure that same sum are not in arrears. In certain instances this can prejudice the creditor, allowing for example a debtor with large judgment debts, who is meeting his regular instalments, to benefit from the sale of a property without paying off the debt.

413.   The Act removes this restriction and enables access to charging orders in circumstances where a debtor is not yet in arrears with an instalment order. As a safeguard, the Act allows the Lord Chancellor to set financial thresholds beneath which a court cannot make a charging order or order for sale, in order to ensure that charging orders are not used to secure payment of disproportionately small judgment debts.

Information requests and orders

414.   Currently, the only means of creditors to obtain information to assist them in determining how to enforce a civil judgment debt is by way of an Order to Obtain Information. This requires the debtor to attend court, which is problematic if the debtor is not co-operating with the court. The Act enables the High Court and the county courts to request information from the DWP and Commissioners for HMRC, other government departments and/or prescribed third parties (including banks and credit reference agencies) on a judgment debtor who has failed to respond to the judgment or comply with court-based methods of enforcement to assist with the enforcement of a judgment debt. Such information will include name, address, date of birth, National Insurance number and the name and address of the debtor's employer.

COMMENTARY ON SECTIONS: PART 4

Section 91: Attachment of earnings orders: deductions at fixed rates

415.   This section and Schedule 15 amend the Attachment of Earnings Act 1971 (the AEA 1971), by making provision for a fixed deductions scheme to introduce deductions from earnings at fixed rates for AEOs made by a county court to secure the payment of a judgment debt.

Schedule 15: Attachment of earnings orders: deductions at fixed rates

416.   This Schedule is in two parts. Part 1 contains the main amendments to the AEA 1971 and inserts new sections and a new Schedule to enable a fixed deductions scheme to operate and to allow for a change in the basis upon which deductions from earnings are made under county court AEOs to secure payment of judgment debts. Part 2 sets out consequential amendments to the AEA 1971.

417.   Paragraph 2 amends section 6 of the AEA 1971 (effect and contents of order) by setting out the basis of deductions from earnings under different AEOs, and specifying that where an AEO is made by a county court to secure payment of a

judgment debt, the AEO must specify that deductions under the order should be made in accordance with the fixed deductions scheme.

418.   Paragraph 3 inserts a new section 6A into the AEA 1971 (the fixed deductions scheme) which defines the fixed deductions scheme and provides for the Lord Chancellor to set out the detail of the scheme in regulations, subject to the affirmative resolution procedure in the first instance. It is intended that such regulations will set out the scheme of deductions in tabular format, in a similar way as is presently used for deductions from earnings for the collection of council tax.

419.   Paragraph 4 amends section 9 of the AEA 1971 (variation, lapse and discharge of orders) by specifying that the power of a court to vary an AEO is subject to Schedule 3A inserted by paragraph 7, which specifies circumstances in which a county court may, and circumstances in which a county court must vary an AEO made to secure the payment of a judgment debt.

420.   Paragraph 5 inserts a new section 9A into the AEA 1971 (suspension of fixed deductions orders), and obliges a county court, in certain circumstances, to suspend an AEO made under the fixed deductions scheme (a fixed deductions order). Where such a suspension order is made, the employer will not have to make deductions from the debtor's earnings and the debtor will make payments directly to the creditor in the manner specified by the court in the suspension order. Where a county court considers that a fixed deductions order is not appropriate (by way of example, because a county court considers that deductions should be more or less than the deductions specified in the fixed deductions scheme because of the personal circumstances of the debtor), it must make a suspension order. The aim of the suspension provisions is to simplify the position for employers (who should only ever have to make deductions from earnings for county court AEOs made to secure a judgment debt in accordance with the fixed deductions scheme). Such a suspension order will specify the rate and timings of repayments by the debtor to the creditor, and might specify other terms. If any of the terms of the suspension order are broken (by way of example, if the debtor fails to make payments to the creditor), then the court must revoke the suspension order and reinstate the AEO (requiring the employer to make deductions from the debtor's earnings). Even where the terms of the suspension order have not been broken, the court may revoke the suspension order if it considers it appropriate to do so, and rules of court may specify the circumstances in which a court may make or revoke a suspension order of its own motion.

421.   Paragraph 7 inserts a new Schedule 3A into the AEA 1971 (changing the basis of deductions). Part 1 of Schedule 3A provides for variations to the basis of deductions under an AEO made to secure a county court judgment debt, such a variation to be changing the basis of deductions from deductions made in accordance with Schedule 3 of the AEA 1971 (a Schedule 3 judgment debt order), to deductions made in accordance with the fixed deductions scheme (a fixed deductions order), therefore, varying an AEO so that the scheme of deductions changes from the current scheme to the new fixed tables scheme. Part 2 of Schedule 3A provides for an AEO made to secure a county court judgment debt to be changed from a fixed deductions order to a Schedule 3 judgment debt order.

422.   Part 1 of Schedule 3A provides that a Schedule 3 judgment debt order can be varied to become a fixed deductions order, either on an application to the county court or of the court's own motion. The court must vary a Schedule 3 judgment debt order

by way of changing it to a fixed deductions order if a Schedule 3 judgment debt order lapses (because the debtor has changed employment) and is then re-directed to the debtor's new employer (such a variation to take effect at the time of re-direction). Paragraph 6 of Schedule 3A enables the Lord Chancellor to specify by order a "changeover date" when all existing Schedule 3 judgment debt orders should become fixed deductions orders. Paragraph 7 of Schedule 3A provides that where an AEO is varied pursuant to Part 1 of Schedule 3A, the employer must comply with the varied order (but will not incur liability for non-compliance until 7 days have elapsed since service of the order as varied).

423.   Part 2 of Schedule 3A deals with changing the basis of deductions under an AEO from a fixed deductions order to a Schedule 3 judgment debt order. Paragraph 10 provides that such a variation can only be made in accordance with Part 2 of Schedule 3A. Paragraph 11 of Schedule 3A specifies that where a county court directs that an existing fixed deductions order should take effect to secure payments under an administration order in accordance with section 5 of the AEA 1971, the AEO must be varied at the same time to specify that deductions under the AEO should be made in accordance with Schedule 3 to the AEA 1971. This is because, for an AEO made to secure payments under an administration order, the county court should retain the flexibility to specify different levels of deductions, and deductions at fixed rates are insufficiently flexible. Paragraph 8 of the Schedule makes a consequential amendment to section 5 of the AEA 1971 to this effect.

424.   Part 2 of the Schedule makes consequential amendments to the AEA 1971 to enable operation of the fixed deductions scheme.

425.   Paragraphs 9 to 15 amend section 14 of the AEA 1971, (power of the court to order the debtor and employer to provide specified information), in connection with the operation of fixed deductions orders to specify that unlike the position in connection with Schedule 3 deductions orders, the court will not need to order the debtor and/or the employer to provide particulars of the debtor's earnings and anticipated earnings, and as to his resources and needs (as the court will not need to be made aware of such facts when it is not setting the level of deductions under the AEO as deductions are to be made in accordance with the fixed deductions scheme). Similarly, paragraph 16 amends section 15 of the AEA 1971 (obligation of debtor and employer to notify changes) to specify that for fixed deductions orders, the debtor and/or the employer are not obliged to notify the court of particulars of earnings or anticipated earnings.

426.   Paragraph 17 makes various consequential amendments in connection with the operation of consolidated attachment orders and paragraph 18 specifies that the fixed deductions scheme should apply to a consolidated attachment order where, before the consolidated order is made, one or more of the AEOs to be consolidated is a Schedule 3 judgment debt order.

Section 92: Attachment of earnings orders: finding the debtor's current employer

427.   This section inserts sections 15A to 15D into the AEA 1971 to enable HMRC information to be provided to the courts for the purpose of re-directing a lapsed AEO.

428.   Section 15A enables the High Court, county courts, magistrates' courts and fines officers, where an AEO has lapsed (where the debtor has changed employment but has failed to notify the court in accordance with his obligations in section 15(a) of

the AEA 1971), to request HMRC to provide the name and address of the debtor's current employer for the purpose of re-directing the AEO. However, no request may be made under this section unless regulations governing the use and supply of debtor information are in force, having been made under section 15B(5) and (8). Section 15A enables HMRC to provide information to comply with a request, disapplies any legal restrictions that might otherwise apply in relation to the disclosure and also enables contractors who hold information on behalf of HMRC to disclose information pursuant to such a request.

429.		Section 15B creates an offence where information obtained pursuant to section 15A is used or disclosed other than for a purpose connected with enforcement of the relevant AEO. Section 15C enables the Lord Chancellor to make regulations under section 15B, with the agreement of the Commissioners and subject to the affirmative resolution procedure. Section 15D sets out various definitions of terms used in sections 15A to 15C.

Section 93: Payment by instalments: making and enforcing charging orders

430.		This section amends the Charging Orders Act 1979 ("the COA 1979") enabling the High Court and county courts to make a charging order in cases where the debtor is not in default under an instalments order made in relation to the sum to be secured by the charging order.

431.		Subsection (3) prevents the court from making an order for sale unless the debtor has defaulted in making any payment due under an instalments order. It also enables rules of court to specify limitations upon enforcement of a charging order after there has been default under an instalments order.

432.		Subsection (5) provides that any restrictions on enforcement of a charge set out in the inserted subsections 3(4A) to (4E) of the COA 1979 will not apply to any charge put on a bankrupt's home under section 313 of the Insolvency Act 1986.

Section 94: Charging orders: power to set financial thresholds

433.		This section inserts a new section 3A into the COA 1979 to provide a power for the Lord Chancellor to specify financial thresholds below which a court cannot make i) a charging order and/or ii) an order for sale. The first of such regulations is to be subject to the affirmative resolution procedure, and any subsequent regulations are to be subject to the negative resolution procedure.

Section 95: Application for information about action to recover judgment debt

434.		This section enables a judgment creditor to apply to the High Court or a county court for information about what type of court based action it would be appropriate to take to recover his debt (an information application), such court-based methods being, for example, a warrant of control, a third party debt order or an AEO.

Section 96: Action by the court

435.		This section enables the High Court or a county court, where the creditor has made an information application, to either make a departmental information request or an information order, requesting or ordering a person to provide information to the court to assist with the creditor's information application. The debtor will be notified that the court intends to make an information request or order to give him an opportunity to object. However, the court may not make a departmental information request to HMRC unless regulations made under section 102(4) and (7) are in force.

They must relate to the use or disclosure of debtor information disclosed by HMRC. Subsection (6) enables the court to disclose information about the debtor to a recipient of an information order or request to enable that recipient to identify the debtor in his records (such information being, for example, the known name and address of the debtor). Subsection (7) disapplies any legal restrictions that might otherwise apply in relation to a disclosure under subsection (6).

Section 97: Departmental information requests

436.   This section specifies the information that may be requested by the court from government departments. Subsection (3) specifies information that may be requested from "the designated Secretary of State" (the Secretary of State for Work and Pensions will be designated for this purpose) and subsection (4) specifies the information that may be requested from HMRC. Subsection (5) enables the court to request prescribed information from other government departments. Such government departments will be requested rather than ordered to provide information and non-legislative agreements will set out arrangements for the respective government departments to deal with such requests.

Section 98: Information orders

437.   This section enables the court to make information orders requiring prescribed third parties to provide prescribed information about the debtor. It is envisaged that credit reference agencies and banks are likely to be recipients of such information orders.

Section 99: Responding to a departmental information request

438.   This section enables a government department in receipt of an information request to disclose information that it considers is necessary to comply with the request and also enables disclosure of information where such information is held by a government contractor. The section disapplies any legal restrictions that might otherwise apply to such a disclosure. Arrangements concerning compliance with such requests will be set out in non-legislative agreements between MoJ and the respective departments.

Section 100: Information order: required information not held etc

439.   This section enables a recipient of an information order (the "information discloser") to avoid liability for failure to comply with the order where the information discloser:

- does not hold the relevant information and it is not being held on his behalf;

- is unable to ascertain whether he holds the information (by way of example, where the information supplied by the court to the recipient of the information order is not sufficient to enable the recipient of the order to identify information that relates to the debtor in its records); or

- would incur an unreasonable effort or expense if he complied with the order.

440.   The information discloser is required to comply with the information order, but may produce a certificate to the relevant court showing that one of the three bullet-points above applies.

Section 101: Using the information about the debtor

441.   This section specifies how information obtained via an information order or departmental information request can be used by the court. Such information can be used by the court:

- to enable it to make a further departmental information request or information order in relation to the debtor (by way of example to further disclose information to enable a recipient of an order or request to identify the debtor more easily from records, such as date of birth information);

- to provide the creditor with information about what court based action he could take to seek to recover his judgment debt;

- to enable a court to take any such action that is initiated by the creditor, by way of example, to enable the court to make and enforce an AEO in relation to the debtor, (and to enable information to be disclosed between courts for the purpose of enforcement).

442.   Regulations will further restrict how information obtained via an information order or request can be further used or disclosed by the court to ensure protection of the debtor's rights and to prevent the unlawful use of information.

Section 102: Offence of unauthorised use or disclosure

443.   This section creates an offence where information obtained pursuant to an information order or request is used or disclosed otherwise than in accordance with the purposes intended.

Section 103: Regulations

444.   This section creates a power for the Lord Chancellor to make regulations relating to sections 95 to 102, with a requirement to seek the agreement of HMRC in relation to any regulations governing the use and disclosure of information disclosed by that Department.

Section 104: Interpretation

445.   This section defines terms used in sections 95 to 103.

Section 105: Application and transitional provision

446.   This section establishes the application of the provisions and sets out the transitional provision.

PART 5: DEBT MANAGEMENT AND RELIEF

SUMMARY

447.   Part 5 of the Act makes changes to two statutory debt-management schemes, Administration Orders (Chapter 1) and Enforcement Restriction Orders (Chapter 2).

448.   Part 5, Chapter 3, also amends the Insolvency Act 1986 to allow for the introduction of a new form of personal insolvency procedure that entails the making, administratively by the official receiver, of a debt relief order (DRO) on the application of an individual debtor who meets specified criteria as regards his assets, income and liabilities. The effect of the order is to stay enforcement of the debts by creditors, the debts being discharged after a period of one year. While the order is in

force, the debtor will be subject to similar restrictions and obligations as if he had been adjudged bankrupt.

449.   Chapter 4 of Part 5 of the Act empowers the Lord Chancellor (or his delegate) to approve Debt Management Schemes ("DMSs") operated by any body of persons. Approved schemes will be able to arrange Debt Repayment Plans ("DRPs") for individual debtors. Subject to prescribed restrictions, schemes will in effect be able to compel creditor participation and plans will be able to compose (i.e. reduce or partially write off) debts. These schemes could be operated by a variety of service providers. Existing providers of debt management advice and assistance do not have the power of compulsion and composition. In future, they will be able to choose whether to offer an 'approved scheme' as part of their service.

450.   It is intended that DRPs will sit alongside and complement statutory schemes, such as Administration Orders ("AOs"), DROs and Individual Voluntary Arrangements ("IVAs"). The intention is to provide a range of options giving more choice and flexibility to assist the rehabilitation of over-indebted people. The most appropriate scheme to use will depend on the particular circumstances.

BACKGROUND

Administration Orders and Enforcement Restriction Orders

451.   Administration Orders ("AOs") are a court-administered debt management scheme for those with multiple debts totalling no more than £5,000, one of which must be a judgment debt. The provisions governing AOs are set out in sections 112-117 of the County Courts Act 1984.

452.   The 1985 Civil Justice Review recommended a number of changes to the AO scheme and these were taken forward in section 13 of the Courts and Legal Services Act 1990 ("the CLSA 1990"). The changes included removal of the need for a judgment debt, an increase in the debt limit and the introduction of a strict three-year limit to the order. Section 13 also included, for the first time, an explicit power for the court to grant an order restricting enforcement where it considered that this would be more appropriate than an AO. Such an order, once made, would provide temporary relief from enforcement for those unable to meet their commitments for a period to be defined by each order. However, as concerns were raised about the viability of section 13, it has never been brought into force.

453.   So, in July 2004 the Government consulted on a range of targeted options to offer better assistance to people with multiple debts (the Choice of Paths Consultation), including reform to the existing AO scheme and a revised and targeted Enforcement Restriction Order ("ERO") scheme. The Government's response paper on the consultation, published in March 2005, committed to a number of changes to the AO scheme including an increase in the debt ceiling and a time limit to orders. The paper also committed to a revised and more workable version of the ERO to address the deficiencies identified in section 13 of the CLSA 1990. Part 5 of the Act takes forward these changes.

Debt Relief Orders

454.   At present if an individual encounters difficulty paying his debts, the remedies that are available to him either require him to have assets or funds available to distribute to his creditors on a regular basis (for example IVA, county court AO or a

non statutory debt management plan) or, as with bankruptcy, there is a fee to access the remedy. This means that the procedures that are currently available are inaccessible to some people, since they do not have the financial means to use them.

455.   Such people often have relatively low levels of liabilities, no assets over and above a nominal amount and no surplus income with which to come to an arrangement with their creditors.

456.   The DRO has been devised following the Choice of Paths consultation, which determined that there was a perceived need for a remedy for people who are financially excluded from the current debt solution procedures, and a further consultation by The Insolvency Service in 2005 ("Relief for the Indebted – an Alternative to Bankruptcy?") on the detail of how it might operate. It is a procedure that will enable some individuals, who meet specified criteria as regards liabilities, assets and income, to seek relief from certain debts.

457.   The DRO will be made administratively by official receivers (who will operate the scheme) and will not routinely require any judicial or other court intervention. The effect of the order will be to prevent creditors from enforcing their debts and the debtor will be discharged from the debts after a period of one year. Creditors will be notified of the making of an order and will have a right to make objections on certain grounds if they believe the order should not have been made.

458.   The debtor will need to pay an up front entry fee to cover the administration costs but this will be significantly less than the deposit required for bankruptcy proceedings to be initiated. In order to keep costs to as low a level as possible, approved intermediaries from the debt advice sector will help an applicant decide if the DRO procedure is right for him before he applies to the official receiver, and assist the debtor in making his application. Again to maintain a low level of administrative costs (and therefore entry fee) the facility to apply for a DRO will be available only online.

459.   To be eligible for an order the debtor will need to meet criteria as regards the level of liabilities, the level of assets and the level of surplus income, and these levels will be set in secondary legislation to enable them to be updated when necessary.

460.   While the order is in force the debtor will be subject to the same restrictions and obligations as in bankruptcy, and will be subject to a similar regime of restrictions orders or prosecution if his conduct in relation to the insolvency is found to be culpable. There will be a right of appeal to the court for both the debtor and creditors who are dissatisfied with the way the official receiver has dealt with the case.

461.   There is a facility to account for windfalls and increases in income during the period when the order is in force.

Debt Management Schemes

462.   Many organisations currently offer advice and assistance to debtors. This can include negotiation with creditors to agree an acceptable schedule of repayments and drawing up plans to help debtors manage their finances and make those repayments. It is estimated that over 25,000 such debt repayment plans were arranged in 2004 and there are currently around 70,000 active plans.

463.   Such schemes depend on the voluntary participation of the debtor and creditors, and operate without any form of regulation. There is currently no power to

compel creditors to adhere to the terms of a debt repayment plan (that is to accept the planned repayments without taking enforcement action). Therefore a single uncooperative creditor can effectively block the creation of a repayment plan that would benefit the debtor and all the other creditors in the long run. Nor is there any power to compose debts that cannot be repaid within a reasonable period as an incentive for the debtor to maintain the required repayments.

464.   Measures in Part 5 of the Act make it clear that business and secured debts cannot be included in these schemes. The measures also enable scheme operators to exercise powers to compel creditor participation, by preventing enforcement action, and to write off a proportion of the debts where a debtor complies with a DRP but simply cannot repay the full amount in a reasonable timescale. Additionally, the measures give the Lord Chancellor power to prescribe in regulations the circumstances in and the extent to which these powers may be exercised. For example, regulations might define the minimum and total repayments for which plans must provide, thereby defining the maximum proportion of the total debts that could be written off. Within these limits, individual schemes could make greater or lesser use of such powers.

465.   The Act also provides creditors with a right of appeal to a county court against the making, their inclusion and terms of a DRP.

466.   Before making regulations to bring this Chapter into effect, the Government intends to undertake further research into existing statutory and non-statutory schemes for assisting the over-indebted and those in multiple debt situations (including the working of the reformed AO scheme). This would inform detailed proposals that would then be subject to a full public consultation exercise and regulatory impact assessment to confirm their benefits and cost effectiveness.

467.   The Choice of Paths consultation sought views on whether it would be desirable in principle for a scheme similar to the court-based AO scheme to be operated in the private and voluntary sectors. A majority of respondents thought that a non-court scheme could offer advantages over the AO scheme. The paper did not discuss the details of such a scheme. The provisions in this Chapter are intended to take powers to give effect to such a scheme or schemes through regulations, subject to further consultation on the details.

COMMENTARY ON SECTIONS: PART 5

Section 106: Administration orders

468.   Subsection (1) of this section replaces the existing Part 6 of the County Court Act 1984 ("CCA 1984").

Section 112A – Administration orders

469.   Section 112A provides that an administration order ("AO") is an order to which certain debts are scheduled, which imposes a requirement on the debtor and which imposes requirements on certain creditors. Debts are to be scheduled to the order in accordance with the provisions in sections 112C, 112D, 112Y(3) and 112Y(4). The requirement which must be imposed on the debtor is set out in section 112E and this is a requirement to make repayments towards scheduled debts whilst the AO is in force. The requirements which must be imposed on certain creditors are

set out in sections 112F to 112I and these are all requirements which restrict the ability of those creditors to take enforcement action whilst an AO is in force.

Section 112B – Power to make order

470.   This section sets out the conditions that must be met before the court can make an AO in relation to a debtor. This is a new test for making AOs which introduces the concept of "qualifying debts" together with other new requirements that must be met before an AO can be obtained. Section 112AB provides that a "qualifying debt" is any debt, except for a debt that is secured against an asset, such as a mortgage, or a debt that falls within a description specified in regulations. The conditions which must be met before an AO can be made are:

- the debtor must have at least two qualifying debts, and he must be unable to pay at least one of them;

- the debtor must not have any business debts;

- the debtor must not be excluded by the AO, voluntary arrangement or bankruptcy exclusions as defined by section 112AH;

- the debtor's total qualifying debts must be less than the amount prescribed in regulations ("the prescribed maximum");

- the debtor's surplus income must be more than the amount prescribed in regulations ("the prescribed minimum").

471.   Section 112AE sets out how "surplus income" is to be calculated. It is to be calculated in accordance with regulations. Before making an AO, the court must have regard to any objections. The Civil Procedure Rules 1998 will govern the procedure for making the order.

Section 112C – Scheduling declared debts

472.   Debtors will be required to declare all qualifying debts, including those which are not due at the time of applying for an order, to ensure that the court has a true picture of their indebtedness. This section provides that when making an AO, the court must schedule to the order all declared debts already due. Declared debts that become due after an AO is made must be scheduled to the order following an application by the debtor or creditor and after considering any objections made to the debt being scheduled (in accordance with section 112AG(5)).

Section 112D – Scheduling new debts

473.   This section gives the court the power to schedule to an existing AO qualifying debts arising after an order is made and becoming due during the life of the order, on the application of the debtor or a qualifying creditor. A "qualifying creditor" is a creditor under a qualifying debt (see section 112AA(1)). However, this power is dependent on the total debt figure (including the new debt) not exceeding the prescribed maximum.

Section 112E – Repayment Requirement

474.   This section imposes a requirement on the debtor to make repayments towards scheduled debts during the life of an AO. Debts may either be repaid in full or to the extent decided by the court and different debts may be repaid to different extents.

475.   Subsection (5) provides the court with the option to order that repayments are not to be made on debts arising after an order is made and scheduled to the order under section 112D, until all of the repayments required in respect of previously declared debts have been made. This provision is designed to discourage irresponsible lending and borrowing.

476.   The section also provides that repayments must be made by instalments and the amount of instalments must be determined in accordance with regulations. The regulations must make provision for instalments to be determined by reference to the debtor's surplus income. The section also allows the court to order repayments to be made by other means, such as by lump sums, in addition to the regular instalments, for example, where the debtor disposes of property.

Section 112F – Presentation of bankruptcy petition

477.   Sections 112F to 112I set out the requirements that must be imposed by an AO on certain creditors for as long as the AO is in force.

478.   The first requirement, in section 112F, provides that any qualifying creditor of the debtor is to be prohibited from presenting a bankruptcy petition against that debtor, unless he has the court's permission. This is similar to the current provision under section 112(4) of the CCA 1984. However, unlike section 112(4), this new section does not include a prohibition on a creditor joining in a bankruptcy petition that has been presented by another creditor. So, if a qualifying creditor obtains the court's permission to present a bankruptcy petition (or if a non-qualifying creditor presents a petition without the court's permission), then all of the debtor's creditors will be able to join in those bankruptcy proceedings. If this leads to the making of a bankruptcy order against the debtor, then the court which made the AO will be required to revoke that AO (see section 112U(4)(b)).

Section 112G – Remedies other than bankruptcy

479.   This section sets out the second requirement that must be imposed by an AO on certain creditors. This is similar to the current provision under section 114 of the CCA 1984. It prohibits qualifying creditors from seeking to recover their debt by pursuing any other remedy (that is, other than bankruptcy) without the court's permission. However, regulations may be made under this section to exempt certain creditors from this requirement in appropriate circumstances. For example, exemptions will apply in respect of debts that are a criminal fine, a student loan or that are due under an order made in family proceedings or maintenance assessments made under the Child Support Act 1991. In relation to these particular types of debt, it is appropriate that the creditor should be free to recover the debt from the debtor, even though an AO is in force. These exceptions will be in line with those categories of debt which are non-provable in bankruptcy proceedings. The revised ERO scheme and the new DRO and DRP schemes will have similar exemptions. This ensures a consistent approach, which is essential to facilitate movement between these schemes for those debtors who need it.

Section 112H – Charging of interest etc.

480.   This section sets out the third requirement that must be imposed by an AO on certain creditors. Any creditor under a scheduled debt is prevented from charging any interest, fee or charge in respect of the scheduled debt during the life of an order.

Section 112I – Stopping supplies of gas or electricity

481.   This section sets out the fourth requirement that must be imposed by an AO on certain creditors – in this case, creditors who are domestic utility suppliers. This largely replicates what would have been section 112A of the CCA 1984, had section 13(5) of the CLSA 1990 been commenced. However, these provisions are limited to imposing restrictions on electricity and gas suppliers because the Water Industry Act 1991 already restricts the powers of water suppliers in relation to domestic supply of water.

Section 112J – Application for an order

482.   Unlike the current provisions, which allow the court to make an order on its own initiative, this new section provides that an AO can only be made on the application of the debtor. It also removes the current need for the debtor to have at least one court judgment in respect of any of his debts. This will ensure that a debtor who needs the protection of an AO is able to obtain an AO without first having to wait for one of his creditors to take him to court.

Section 112K – Duration

483.   This section differs from the current legislation by setting a maximum overall limit of 5 years on the duration of an AO. At present, AOs are not time limited. Section 112(9) of the CCA 1984, which was to be inserted into that Act by section 13(4) of the CLSA 1990 had it been commenced, limited AOs to a maximum period of 3 years. An order will cease to have effect 5 years after the date on which it was made, unless the court has specified an earlier date in the order. If the court specifies an earlier date when it makes the AO, then it may subsequently extend the length of that order under section 112S (variation of duration), provided that the overall length remains within the 5 year time limit from the making of the order. The court may also revoke an AO before it is due to expire, under section 112U or section 112V (duty and power to revoke order), and in those cases the order will cease to have effect in accordance with the revocation.

484.   The intention is to make the AO scheme more effective by providing certainty about the length of the order, as well as an opportunity for a debtor's rehabilitation (because of the fixed term), a reasonable return to creditors and an incentive to maintain the repayments.

Section 112L – Effect on other debt management arrangements

485.   This new section defines the relationship between an AO and the other debt management arrangements set out in subsection (6), which are EROs, DROs and DRPs. It provides that when an AO is made, any other debt management arrangement which had effect in relation to the same debtor immediately before it was made will cease to have effect automatically when the AO is made. Provision is also made for the court to notify the provider of the other arrangements as soon as practicable, or as soon as it becomes aware of their existence, of the making of the AO. Similar provisions are incorporated into the revised ERO scheme and the new DRO and DRP schemes This will ensure that no more than one debt management arrangement has effect in respect of the same debtor at the same time.

Section 112M – Duty to provide information

486.   This new section applies as long as an AO is in force and requires a debtor, who is the subject of an AO, to supply information about his earnings and income (including, for example, any cash that he might win or receive as a gift) and his assets and expenditure at intervals to be specified in regulations. The information to be provided must include details of any anticipated changes that are likely to occur before the next statement is due, for example if the debtor knows that he is due to receive a bonus in his next pay. Additionally, debtors will be required to notify the court within a period, again to be specified in regulations (probably 7 – 14 days), before he disposes of any property (including cash) that is above a set value, to be specified in regulations.

487.   This new provision is intended to facilitate the court's role in actively managing an AO, for example by exercising its powers to vary or revoke the order where appropriate.

Section 112N – Offence if information not provided

488.   This section provides that any failure to provide information, as required under section 112M, is an offence which is punishable by a county court judge who may impose a fine of not more than £250 or imprisonment for not more than 14 days. This offence is not a criminal offence; instead it is treated as if it were a contempt of court. The penalty is equivalent to that which applies to a debtor who fails to provide the information required by section 15 of the Attachment of Earnings Act 1971 (see section 23 of that Act).

Section 112O – Existing county court proceedings to be stayed

489.   This section provides that any county court proceedings that were pending against the debtor when the AO was made, must be stayed if the following conditions apply:

- the proceedings relate to one of the debtor's qualifying debts and they are not bankruptcy proceedings;

- following the making of the AO, the creditor under that debt is unable to enforce it because of the prohibition referred to in section 112G (remedies other than bankruptcy); and

- the county court, in the proceedings which are to be stayed, has notice of the AO.

490.   Where proceedings are stayed under this section, the county court has discretion to allow the creditor any costs incurred in the stayed proceedings. Those costs may be added to the qualifying debt or, if the debt is scheduled to the AO, to the amount scheduled in respect of the debt but only if the court is not under a duty to revoke the order because the total qualifying debts, including the costs, exceeds the prescribed maximum (see section 112U(6)(b)).

Section 112P – Appropriation of money paid

491.   This section provides that monies paid by a debtor under an AO will first be appropriated towards court fees and then towards the debts scheduled to the order. So, a debtor need not pay the court fees up front; instead, they can be paid from the monies the debtor pays to the court under the AO.

Section 112Q – Discharge from debts

492.   This section places a duty on the court to discharge the debtor from a scheduled debt and to de-schedule the debt where the debt is repaid to the extent provided in the order, even if the debt is not repaid to its full extent. Once all of the scheduled debts have been repaid to the extent required by the order, then the court must revoke that order.

Section 112R – Variation

493.   This section provides that the court may vary an AO on its own initiative or on the application of either the debtor or a qualifying creditor. This provision allows the court to take a more pro-active role in the management of the order by being able to react to information received from the debtor under section 112M.

Section 112S – Variation of duration

494.   This section makes provision to allow the court to vary the duration of an AO. So, for example, an AO that was due to come to an end after 5 years from the day it was made can be shortened so that instead it comes to an end after 4 years from the day it was made. Similarly, an AO that was due to come to an end after 3 years, can be extended so that it continues to have effect for a further 2 years. But the overall duration of an AO (including any extensions under this section) must not exceed a period of 5 years from the day it was made.

Section 112T – De-scheduling debts

495.   This new section enables the court to use its power of variation under section 112R to vary an administration order by de-scheduling the debt, if it appears to the court that it is just and equitable to do so. This will normally be when debts have been incorrectly scheduled to an order.

Section 112U – Duty to revoke order

496.   This section makes provision for the revocation of an order on specified grounds. It places a duty on the court to revoke an AO if it becomes apparent that at the time the order was made, or subsequently, the entry criteria in section 112B were not or are no longer met. That is where the debtor:

- did not have two or more qualifying debts/does not have any qualifying debts;

- had/has a business debt and in either case he is still a debtor under that debt;

- was excluded under the AO, voluntary arrangement or insolvency exclusions (as defined in section 112AH), is now excluded under the voluntary arrangement exclusion or is now the subject of a bankruptcy order;

- was/is now able to pay all of his qualifying debts;

- had/has total qualifying debts exceeding the prescribed maximum; and

- had/has surplus income less than or the same as the prescribed minimum.

Section 112V – Power to revoke order

497.   This section gives the court, on its own motion or on the application of either the debtor or a qualifying creditor, a general power to revoke an AO in circumstances where it does not have a duty to do so. This power may be used particularly where a

debtor fails to make two payments (whether consecutive or not) required by the order under section 112E or fails to provide information required under section 112M.

Section 112W – Effect of Revocation

498.   This section confirms that if an order is revoked under a duty or power in this Part, then it ceases to have effect in accordance with the terms of the revocation.

Section 112X – Notice when order made, varied, revoked etc

499.   This section imposes a duty on the court to send notice to all creditors with scheduled debts if and when the following things happen:

- when an AO is made, varied or revoked;

- when a debt is scheduled to the order at any time after it is made;

- when the court itself is given notice that another debt management arrangement has been made (with the consequence that the AO has ceased to have effect automatically).

Section 112Y – Failure to take account of all qualifying debts

500.   This section places a duty on the court to schedule an undeclared debt to an AO if the following conditions apply:

- an AO has been made but because of an undeclared debt, the total amount of the debtor's qualifying debts was not properly calculated;

- the undeclared debt is due, whether or not it became due before or after the AO was made; and

- the total debt is less than or the same as the prescribed maximum.

501.   If the undeclared debt is not yet due, the court must schedule the debt to the order when it becomes due. Where the inclusion of the debt would result in the total debt exceeding the prescribed maximum, the court must instead revoke the order.

502.   nder this section, the court must take account of any representations (including representations about why a debt should not be scheduled) in accordance with section 112AG(5)).

Section 112AA – Main definitions

503.   This section explains the meaning of key expressions used in this Part. In particular, it confirms that the terms "administration order" and "debtor" have the meanings given to them in new sections 112A and 112B, respectively. It also defines "qualifying creditor" as a creditor under a qualifying debt and confirms that, subject to the normal rules of court, "proper county court" refers to the court that made the order.

Section 112AB – Expressions relating to debts

504.   This section defines a "qualifying debt" as any debt that is not secured against an asset or specified in regulations. A "business debt" is defined as a debt incurred in the course of a business. This section confirms that references to debts include only those debts that have arisen and therefore contingent debts are not included.

Section 112AC – Inability to pay debts

505. This section specifies that a debtor is considered to be unable to repay a debt if, when the debt is due, he fails to pay it (if the debt is repayable by a single payment) or, he fails to make one or more payments (if the debt is repayable by a number of instalments) and is unable to pay the single payment or all of the missed payments.

Section 112AD – Calculating the debtor's qualifying debts

506. This section requires the court to calculate the total amount of a debtor's qualifying debts by taking into account all qualifying debts that have arisen before the calculation, including those which are not due to be paid at the time of the calculation (that is, where payment is deferred). This ensures that the court is aware of the true extent of a debtor's indebtedness. In addition, the section requires regulations to make further provision about how the total amount of a debtor's qualifying debts is to be calculated and enables regulations to make provision about how the amount of any particular qualifying debt is to be calculated.

Section 112AE – Calculating the debtor's surplus income

507. This section requires the debtor's surplus income to be calculated in accordance with regulations which must make provision about what is surplus income (this is likely to be the difference between average income, over a specific period, and justifiable expenditure) and the period by reference to which the debtor's surplus income is to be calculated. The regulations may allow the court to take into account the debtor's assets, such as his savings, when calculating his surplus income.

Section 112AF – Debts becoming due

508. This section specifies when a debt, which is repayable by a single repayment or by a number of payments, becomes due. The debt becomes due when the time for making the single payment or the first of the payments is reached.

Section 112AG – Scheduling and de-scheduling debts

509. This section explains when a debt is scheduled to and de-scheduled from an AO. If the amount of the debt and the name of the creditor under the debt is included in a schedule to the order, the debt is scheduled to the order. The debt is de-scheduled when this information is removed from the schedule. The court must not schedule or de-schedule a debt without having regard to any representations from any person about why the debt should not be scheduled or de-scheduled. However, where an undeclared debt is scheduled under section 112Y, the court need not have regard to any representations made by a debtor about the scheduling of that debt. Also, where a debt is de-scheduled because a debtor is discharged from his debt under section 112Q, the court need not have regard to any representations made by any person.

Section 112AH – The AO, voluntary arrangement and bankruptcy exclusions

510. This section defines the AO, voluntary arrangement and bankruptcy exclusions, which are relevant to the court's power to make an AO (see section 112B(4)). It specifies that a debtor is excluded under the:

- ***AO Exclusion*** if he currently has an AO, or he previously had an AO within the last 12 months. For this purpose, the 12-month period begins on the day that the previous AO ceased to have effect. But a debtor who has had an AO within the last 12 months is not excluded under this provision if the previous

AO (a) ceased to have effect by virtue of another debt management arrangement listed in section 112K(7) coming into force, or (b) was revoked for the reason that the debtor no longer had any qualifying debts (see section 112U(1)(b));

- *Voluntary Arrangement Exclusion* if the debtor is the subject of an interim order under section 252 of the Insolvency Act 1986 (interim court order pending an individual voluntary arrangement) or where he is bound by an individual voluntary arrangement approved under Part 8 of that Act;

- *Bankruptcy Exclusion* if a petition under Part 9 of the Insolvency Act 1986 has been presented in respect of the debtor but has not yet been decided, or if the debtor is an undischarged bankrupt.

Section 112AI – Regulations under this Part

511.   This section provides the Lord Chancellor with powers to make regulations under this Part.

512.   Subsection (2) of this section enacts Schedule 16.

Schedule 16: Administration orders: consequential amendments

513.   This Schedule contains a number of amendments to numerous Acts which are consequential as result of the new provisions in Part 6 of the CCA 1984.

514.   Subsection (3) of this section specifies that the application of the new provisions do not apply where an AO was made or an application for an AO was made before the day on which the new provisions come into force.

Section 107: Enforcement restriction orders

515.   Subsection (1) of this section inserts a new Part 6A into the CCA 1984.

Section 117A – Enforcement Restriction Orders

516.   Section 117A provides that an enforcement restriction order ("ERO") is an order which imposes requirements on certain creditors and which may also impose a requirement on the debtor. The requirements which must be imposed on certain creditors are set out in sections 117C to 117E and these are all requirements which restrict the ability of those creditors to take enforcement action whilst an ERO is in force. The requirement which may be imposed on the debtor is set out in section 117F and this is a requirement to make repayments towards certain debts whilst the ERO is in force.

Section 117B – Power to make order

517.   This section sets out the conditions that must be met before the court can make an enforcement restriction order in relation to a debtor. This is a new test for making EROs, which introduces the concept of "qualifying debts" together with other new requirements that must be met before an ERO can be obtained. Section 117T provides that a "qualifying debt" is any debt, except for a debt that is secured against an asset, such as a mortgage, or a debt that falls within a description specified in regulations. The conditions which must be met before an ERO can be made are:

- the debtor must have at least two qualifying debts, and he must be unable to pay at least one of them;

- the debtor must not have any business debts;

- the debtor must not be excluded by the ERO, voluntary arrangement or bankruptcy exclusions as defined by section 117W;

- the debtor must be suffering from a sudden and unforeseen deterioration in his financial circumstances from which there must be a realistic prospect of improvement in financial terms within 6 months from when the order is made.

518.   The Civil Procedure Rules 1998 ("CPR") will govern the procedure for making the order. It is intended that the court should be able to make the order without first giving notice to the creditors. For that reason, section 117B(10) allows the CPR to disapply the requirement for the court to consider any objections before making an order. However, the court will be required to have regard to any objections that a creditor may have after the order has been made and may vary or revoke the order if appropriate, in the light of those objections.

117C – Presentation of bankruptcy petition

519.   Sections 117C to 117E set out the requirements that must be imposed by an ERO on certain creditors for as long as the ERO is in force. The first requirement, in section 117C, provides that any qualifying creditor of the debtor is to be prohibited from presenting a bankruptcy petition against that debtor, unless he has the court's permission. This is similar to the current provision under section 112(4) of the CCA 1984 which applies to administration orders ("AOs"). However, unlike section 112(4), this new section does not include a prohibition on a creditor joining in a bankruptcy petition that has been presented by another creditor. So if a qualifying creditor obtains the court's permission to present a bankruptcy petition (or if a non-qualifying creditor presents a petition without the court's permission), then all of the debtor's creditors will be able to join in those bankruptcy proceedings. If this leads to the making of a bankruptcy order against the debtor, then the court which made the ERO will be required to revoke that ERO (see section 117O(4)(b)). A "qualifying creditor" is a creditor under a qualifying debt (see section 117T(1)).

Section 117D – Remedies other than bankruptcy

520.   This section sets out the second requirement that must be imposed by an ERO on certain creditors. It re-enacts in part what would have been section 112A(2) of the CCA 1984, which was to be inserted by section 13(5) of the CLSA 1990 had it been commenced. This second requirement prohibits qualifying creditors from seeking to recover their debt by pursuing any other remedy (that is, other than bankruptcy) without the court's permission. However, in contrast to section 112(4) of the CCA 1984, regulations may be made under this section to exempt certain creditors from this requirement in appropriate circumstances. For example, exemptions will apply in respect of debts that are a criminal fine, a student loan or that are due under an order made in family proceedings or maintenance assessments made under the Child Support Act 1991. In relation to these particular types of debt, it is appropriate that the creditor should be free to recover the debt from the debtor, even though an ERO is in force. These exceptions will be in line with those categories of debt which are non-provable in bankruptcy proceedings. The revised AO scheme and the new DRO and DRP schemes will have similar exemptions. This ensures a consistent approach, which is essential to facilitate movement between these schemes for those debtors who need it.

Section 117E – Stopping supplies of gas or electricity

521.　This section sets out the third requirement that must be imposed by an ERO on certain creditors, in this case creditors who are domestic utility suppliers. Again this largely replicates what would have been section 112A of the County Court Act 1984, had section 13(5) of the CLSA 1990 been commenced. However, these provisions are limited to imposing restrictions on electricity and gas suppliers because the Water Industry Act 1991 already restricts the powers of water suppliers in relation to domestic supply of water.

Section 117F – Repayment requirement

522.　This section sets out the requirement that may be imposed by an ERO on the debtor. This gives the court discretion to order the debtor to make payments towards one or more of his qualifying debts, whilst the ERO is in force, provided that the debtor has sufficient surplus income. Regulations will make provision about what is surplus income (which is likely to be the difference between average income and justifiable expenditure, in common with the AO provisions) and specifies that assets, such as the debtor's savings, may be taken into account when making this calculation. It also allows the court to vary the repayment requirement of its own initiative or on the application of the debtor or a qualifying creditor.

Section 117G – Application for an order

523.　This section specifies that only a debtor can apply for an ERO and that a debtor can make an application regardless of whether any of his creditors has obtained a court judgment in respect of any of his debts. (Under the current provisions in the CCA 1984, a judgment debt is a precondition to the court making an AO or ERO). This will ensure that a debtor who needs the protection of an ERO is able to obtain an ERO without first having to wait for one of his creditors to take him to court.

Section 117H – Duration

524.　This section provides for a maximum overall time limit of 12 months on the duration of an ERO. An order will cease to have effect 12 months after the date on which it was made, unless the court has specified an earlier date in the order. If the court specifies an earlier date when it makes the ERO, then it may subsequently extend the length of that order under section 117N (variation of duration), provided that the overall length remains within the 12 month time limit from the making of the order. The court may also revoke an ERO before it was due to expire, under section 117O or section 117P (duty and power to revoke order), and in those cases the order will cease to have effect in accordance with the revocation.

Section 117I – Effect on other debt management arrangements

525.　This new section defines the relationship between an ERO and the other debt management arrangements set out in subsection (6), which are AOs, DROs and DRPs. It provides that, when an ERO is made, any other debt management arrangement which had effect in relation to the same debtor immediately before it was made will cease to have effect automatically when the ERO is made. Provision is also made for the court to notify the provider of the other arrangements as soon as practicable, or as soon as it becomes aware of their existence, of the making of the ERO. Similar provisions are incorporated into the revised AO scheme and the new DRO and DRP schemes. This will ensure that no more than one debt management arrangement has effect in respect of the same debtor at the same time.

Section 117J – Duty to provide information

526.   This new section applies as long as an ERO is in force and requires a debtor, who is the subject of an ERO, to supply information about his earnings and income (including, for example, any cash that he might win or receive as a gift) and his assets and expenditure at intervals to be specified in regulations. The information to be provided must include details of any anticipated changes that are likely to occur before the next statement is due, for example if the debtor knows that he is due to receive a bonus in his next pay. Additionally, debtors will be required to notify the court within a period, again to be specified in regulations (probably 7 – 14 days), before he disposes of any property (including cash) that is above a set value, to be specified in regulations.

527.   This new provision is intended to facilitate the court's role in actively managing an ERO, for example by exercising its powers to vary or revoke the order where appropriate.

Section 117K Offence if information not provided

528.   This section provides that any failure to provide information, as required under section 117J, is an offence which is punishable by a county court judge who may impose a fine of not more than £250 or imprisonment for not more than 14 days. This offence is not a criminal offence; instead it is treated as if it were a contempt of court. The penalty is equivalent to that which applies to a debtor who fails to provide the information required by section 15 of the Attachment of Earnings Act 1971 (see section 23 of that Act).

Section 117L – Existing county court proceedings to be stayed

529.   This section provides that any county court proceedings, that were pending against the debtor when the ERO was made, must be stayed if the following conditions apply:

- the proceedings relate to one of the debtor's qualifying debts and they are not bankruptcy proceedings;

- following the making of the ERO, the creditor under that debt is unable to enforce it because of the prohibition referred to in section 117D (remedies other than bankruptcy); and

- the county court, in the proceedings which are to be stayed, has notice of the ERO.

530.   Where proceedings are stayed under this section, the county court has discretion to allow the creditor any costs incurred in the stayed proceedings and those costs may be added to the qualifying debt.

Section 117M – Charges

531.   This new provision prohibits qualifying creditors from making any charge, other than interest or charges relating to issues before an ERO came into existence, for the period while an ERO is or was in force. So the prohibition remains in place even after the ERO has ceased to have effect. This provision is designed to prevent creditors, who are prohibited from enforcing their debts whilst an ERO has effect,

from penalising the debtor under the ERO by imposing additional penalty charges or interest for his late payment of the relevant debt. If the creditor tries to impose any such charge, in breach of this section, then that charge will be unenforceable.

Section 117N – Variation of duration

532.   This section makes provision to allow the court, on its own initiative or on the application of the debtor or a qualifying creditor, to vary the duration of an ERO. So, for example, an ERO that was due to come to an end after 12 months can be shortened so that instead it comes to an end after 8 months from the day it was made. Similarly, an ERO that was due to come to an end after 6 months, can be extended so that it continues to have effect for a further 3 months. But the overall duration of an ERO (including any extensions under this section) must not exceed a period of 12 months from the day it was made.

Section 117O – Duty to revoke order

533.   This section makes provision for the revocation of an order on specified grounds. It places a duty on the court to revoke an ERO if it becomes apparent that at the time that the order was made, or subsequently, the entry criteria in section 117B were not or are no longer met. That is where the debtor:

- did not have two or more qualifying debts/does not have any qualifying debts;

- had/has a business debt and in either case he is still a debtor under that debt;

- was excluded under the ERO, voluntary arrangement or insolvency exclusions (as defined in section 117W), is now excluded under the voluntary arrangement exclusion or is now the subject of a bankruptcy order;

- was/ is now able to pay all of his qualifying debts;

- was not/is no longer suffering from a sudden and unforeseen deterioration in his financial circumstances; and

- did not have/no longer has realistic prospects of improvement in his financial circumstances.

534.   Additionally, the court must revoke an ERO if it becomes apparent that at the time the order was made it was not in fact fair and equitable to make the order or where it is not now fair and equitable for the order to continue to have effect.

Section 117P – Power to revoke order

535.   This section gives the court, on its own motion or on the application of either the debtor or a qualifying creditor, a general power to revoke an ERO in circumstances where it does not have a duty to do so. This power may be used particularly where a debtor fails to comply with a repayment requirement that is (or was) included in the order under section 117F or fails to provide information required under section 117J.

Section 117Q – Effect of revocation

536.   This section confirms that if an order is revoked under a duty or power in this Part, then it ceases to have effect in accordance with the terms of the revocation.

Section 117R – Notice of order

537.   This section imposes a duty on the court to send notice to all qualifying creditors if and when the following things happen:

- when an ERO is made, varied or revoked;

- when the court itself is given notice that another debt management arrangement has been made (with the consequence that the ERO has ceased to have effect automatically).

Section 117T – Main definitions

538.   This section explains the meaning of key expressions used in this Part. In particular, it confirms that the terms "enforcement restriction order" and "debtor" have the meanings given to them in new sections 117A and 117B, respectively. It also defines "qualifying creditor" as a creditor under a qualifying debt and confirms that, subject to the normal rules of court, "proper county court" refers to the court that made the order.

Section 117U – Expressions relating to debts

539.   This section defines a "qualifying debt" as any debt that is not secured against an asset or specified in regulations. A "business debt" is defined as a debt incurred in the course of a business. This section confirms that references to debts include only those debts that have arisen and therefore contingent debts are not included.

Section 117V – Inability to pay debts

540.   This section specifies that a debtor is considered to be unable to repay a debt if, when the debt is due, he fails to pay it (if the debt is repayable by a single payment) or, he fails to make one or more payments (if the debt is repayable by a number of instalments) and is unable to pay the single payment or all of the missed payments.

Section 117W – The ERO, voluntary arrangement and bankruptcy exclusions

541.   This section defines the ERO, voluntary arrangement and bankruptcy exclusions, which are relevant to the court's power to make an ERO (see section 117B(4)). It specifies that a debtor is excluded under the:

- ***ERO Exclusion*** if he currently has an ERO, or he previously had an ERO within the last 12 months. For this purpose, the 12-month period begins on the day that the previous ERO ceased to have effect. But a debtor who has had an ERO within the last 12 months is not excluded under this provision if the previous ERO (a) ceased to have effect by virtue of another debt management arrangement listed in section 117H(7) coming into force, or (b) was revoked for the reason that the debtor no longer had any qualifying debts (see section 117O(1)(b));

- ***Voluntary Arrangement Exclusion*** if the debtor is the subject of an interim order under section 252 of the Insolvency Act 1986 (interim court order pending an individual voluntary arrangement) or where he is bound by an individual voluntary arrangement approved under Part 8 of that Act;

- ***Bankruptcy Exclusion*** if a petition under Part 9 of the Insolvency Act 1986 has been presented in respect of the debtor but has not yet been decided, or if the debtor is an undischarged bankrupt.

Section 117X – Power to make regulations

542.   This section empowers the Lord Chancellor to make regulations under this Part.

Section 108: Debt relief orders and debt relief restrictions orders etc

543.   Section 108 gives effect to Schedules 17, 18 and 19 and makes provision for the addition of a new Part 7A of the Insolvency Act 1986 and additional Schedules (Schedule 4ZA on the conditions to be met for a DRO and Schedule 4ZB relating to debt relief restrictions orders) to that Act. These provisions relate to the operation of a new individual insolvency procedure, the debt relief order ("DRO").

Schedule 17 – Part 7A to the Insolvency Act 1986

544.   Schedule 17 contains the text of new Part 7A to be inserted into the Insolvency Act 1986.

Section 251A: Debt Relief Orders

545.   Only individuals who are unable to pay their debts may apply for a debt relief order. The section also identifies the debts to which a DRO may apply - which are called "qualifying debts" in the Act. The debts must be for an identifiable amount of money and must not be secured or within any description of debt that may be prescribed by order as being excluded from being a qualifying debt.

Section 251B: Making of application

546.   Section 251B provides for the way in which the debtor must apply to the official receiver for an order. The application must be made through an approved intermediary. The term "approved intermediary" is defined later in section 251U. The section sets out some of the detail about the individual's affairs that must be included in an application for a DRO, and makes provision for the individual insolvency rules made under section 412 to prescribe the form and manner in which the application should be made and the information that must be supplied in support of the application.

Section 251C: Duty of official receiver to consider and determine application

547.   Once an application has been made the official receiver must decide whether to make, refuse or stay the application pending further enquiries. This section describes the steps the official receiver should take when an application for a DRO has been made. It allows the official receiver to stay his consideration of the application until he receives answers to any queries raised by him with the debtor.

548.   The section sets out the circumstances in which the official receiver must refuse the application (if he is not satisfied that the debtor meets the criteria for a DRO) and also that he may refuse it if the application does not satisfy the requirements imposed by section 251B or if queries raised with the debtor have not been answered to the official receiver's satisfaction. If the official receiver refuses the application he must give reasons to the debtor. If he does not refuse the application then he must make the order.

Section 251D: Presumptions applicable to the determination of an application

549.   In order to ensure that there is a uniform approach to the order making process and that the great majority of applications can be decided quickly, the official receiver

must apply certain presumptions when determining an application for a DRO. This section requires him to presume that the debtor meets the requirements for a DRO if it appears to be the case from information supplied in the application and he has no reason to believe that the information supplied is inaccurate or that the debtor's circumstances have changed since the application date.

550.   The official receiver must also presume that the debtor meets the conditions as to eligibility as set out in Schedule 4ZA providing he has no reason to believe that incomplete or inaccurate information has been supplied in the application or in support of it. The official receiver may also presume that the debts specified at the date of the application are qualifying debts unless he has reason to believe otherwise.

551.   It is expected that the involvement of authorised intermediaries in filling in and submitting application forms means that most applications will be well-founded. This section allows the official receiver to make orders where the application appears to be in order without considering the case in any more detail. However, where an objection is made to the order or for any reason the official receiver discovers that the order arguably should not have been made, the official receiver will be expected to look into the case in far more detail. That is thought to provide adequate protection for creditors and will ensure that the administrative costs, and hence the application fees, can be kept as low as possible.

Section 251E: Making of debt relief orders

552.   This section makes provision for the form of the DRO, including some of the matters that must be included in the order, for example a list of the debtor's qualifying debts and entry of its details on the individual insolvency register provided for by the Insolvency Act 1986. It also makes provision for the steps that the official receiver must take once the order has been made, including providing a copy of the order to the debtor, and allows for rules to prescribe other steps he must take in particular with regard to notifying creditors and informing them of the grounds on which they may object.

Section 251F: Effect of debt relief order on other debt management arrangements

553.   This section provides that where a DRO is made, any debt management arrangements, as defined, that were in place at the time will cease to be in force.

Section 251G: Moratorium from qualifying debts

554.   Section 251G further sets out the effect of a DRO. Once the order is entered onto the register, a moratorium in respect of the debts specified in the order takes effect. During the moratorium creditors specified in the order are prohibited from taking proceedings to enforce the debt or present a bankruptcy petition in relation to that debt, except with leave of the court.

Section 251H: The moratorium period

555.   In most cases, the moratorium period is one year from the date of entry on the register. However, the order may be terminated early for example if the debtor's financial circumstances change such that he can make arrangements to pay his creditors, or if he has been found to have provided misleading information on his application.

556.   The section makes provision for the moratorium period to be extended by the official receiver or the court and the circumstances in which an extension is permitted.

Such circumstances include carrying out or completing an investigation into the debtor's affairs (only with the permission of the court) or providing the debtor with the opportunity to make arrangements to pay his creditors before revoking the order.

Section 251I: Discharge from qualifying debts

557.   Section 251I provides for the debtor to be discharged from his qualifying debts specified in the order at the end of the moratorium period, and the circumstances in which the debtor will not be discharged from the debts – in particular if the moratorium period is terminated early. The debtor will not be discharged from any debts listed in the order that were incurred through fraud. The section also specifies that discharge of the debtor from the debts does not release any other person from their liability for the debts.

Section 251J: providing assistance to official receiver etc

558.   This section sets out the requirements imposed on the debtor with regard to assisting the official receiver in carrying out his functions. It requires the debtor to provide the official receiver with information about his affairs and attend on the official receiver. The requirement extends so far as the official receiver may reasonably require in order to carry out his functions in relation to the application or the debt relief order made as a result of it. The debtor is also under a duty to notify the official receiver of changes in his circumstances during and before the moratorium period. He must also notify the official receiver if he becomes aware of any errors or omissions in his application.

Section 251K: Objections and Investigations

559.   Creditors are permitted to object to the making of the order on specified grounds and this section makes provision for that. In particular, the section makes provision for any person specified in the order as a creditor to object to the making of the order or his inclusion in the order or to details of the debt specified. It also gives details of how the objection must be made and requires the official receiver to consider the objection. It allows the official receiver to carry out an investigation if it seems appropriate and gives a power to the official receiver to require any person to give him information and assistance.

Section 251L: Power of official receiver to revoke or amend a debt relief order

560.   This section sets out the circumstances in which the official receiver may revoke the order and gives him a power to amend the order during the moratorium period to correct errors and omissions. Revocation may take place when information provided by the debtor to the official receiver turns out to be incomplete or misleading, or where the debtor fails to comply with his duties to provide information or attend on the official receiver. The order may also be revoked if the official receiver ought not have made the order because he ought not have been satisfied the criteria were met and also if the debtor's income and property levels change (for example following a windfall) after the order has been made and the debtor would no longer meet the criteria for obtaining an order.

Section 251M: Powers of court in relation to debt relief orders

561.   This section enables persons who are dissatisfied with the actions of the official receiver to apply to the court and for the court to give directions or make any order it thinks fit. It also enables the official receiver to make an application for

directions or an order in relation to any matter arising in connection with the DRO or an application for a DRO. An application to the court may, subject to anything contained in the rules, be made at any time.

Section 251N: Inquiry into debtor's dealings and property

562.   This section enables the court, on the application of the official receiver, to require the debtor, the debtor's spouse, former spouse, civil partner or former civil partner or any person appearing to be able to give information or assistance to the court to appear before the court. There are sanctions for failure to appear without reasonable excuse – the court may issue a warrant for the person's arrest or order the seizure of books, papers and other items. It is not expected that there will be a frequent use of this power, which is aimed at a very small number of cases where misconduct – for example the hiding of assets – is suspected and the debtor has refused to provide information to the official receiver.

Section 251O: False representations and omissions

563.   In order that the official receiver can determine whether a DRO should be made, the debtor must provide complete and accurate information about his affairs. Similarly, the debtor remains under an obligation to provide information to the Official Receiver once the DRO is made. This section provides that a debtor who deliberately provides false information or omits pertinent information commits an offence.

Section 251P: Concealment or falsification of documents

564.   This section provides that a failure to produce books, papers or other documents to the official receiver is an offence. Similarly, preventing such records being produced, or their concealment, destruction or falsification will also be an offence. The offence may be committed before the application for the DRO has been made, and during both the application process and the moratorium period, and it is irrelevant that the order may have been revoked subsequent to an offence being committed.

Section 251Q: Fraudulent disposal of property

565.   In order to meet the eligibility criteria for a DRO, the debtor must meet various conditions including a limit on the value of property he owns. A debtor who disposes of property, whether in an attempt to meet the eligibility criteria or to deny creditors access to that property, is clearly acting in an inappropriate manner. The section ensures that a debtor who obtains a DRO is guilty of an offence if he fraudulently disposes of any property during the two years before the application date or during the moratorium period. It is irrelevant that the order may have been revoked subsequent to an offence being committed.

Section 251R: Fraudulent dealing with property obtained on credit

566.   This section makes it an offence if the debtor disposes of property obtained on credit for which he has not paid, and similarly penalises the knowing recipient of such property. No offence is committed if the disposal or acquisition was in the ordinary course of the debtor's business, but particular attention will be paid to the price paid for the property. The offence may be committed before the application for the DRO has been made, and during the application process.

Section 251S: Obtaining credit or engaging in business

567.   This section makes it an offence for the debtor to obtain credit (either alone or jointly with another person) to the extent of a prescribed amount, or to trade in a name other than that which the DRO was made, without disclosing his status. His status is that there is a moratorium is in force in relation to his qualifying debts by virtue of a DRO or that there is a debt relief restrictions order in force in relation to him. Subsection (5) specifies that "obtaining credit" includes obtaining goods under a hire purchase agreement and also payment in advance for the supply of goods and services.

Section 251T: Offences: supplementary

568.   This section sets out who may institute proceedings for an offence under this Part and the penalties imposed on a person who commits such an offence. The section also makes it clear it is not a defence that the conduct complained of was done outside England and Wales.

Section 251U: Approved intermediaries

569.   In order to obtain a debt relief order, the debtor must make his application to the official receiver through an approved intermediary. This section defines an approved intermediary and makes provision for rules to specify the types of activities that should be undertaken by an intermediary.

570.   It also states that authorisation will be granted by a competent authority designated by the Secretary of State to grant authorisations, and allows for regulations to make provision as to the procedure for designating persons to be competent authorities, the types of persons who may not be authorised to act as approved intermediaries, the procedure for dealing with applications to competent authorities for authorisation and the withdrawal of designation to act as a competent authority.

Section 251V: Debt relief restrictions orders and undertakings

571.   This section gives effect to Schedule 4ZB, which makes provision about debt relief restrictions orders. Such orders will be very similar in operation and effect as the existing bankruptcy restriction orders.

Section 251W: Register of debt relief orders etc

572.   Section 251W requires the Secretary of State to establish and maintain a register of DROs, debt relief restrictions orders and debt relief restriction undertakings.

Section 251X: Interpretation

573.   This section defines the meaning of various expressions used in this Part of the Insolvency Act 1986.

Schedule 18: Schedule 4ZA to the Insolvency Act 1986

574.   Schedule 18 contains the text of new Schedule 4ZA to be inserted into the Insolvency Act 1986. Schedule 4ZA sets out the conditions for making a debt relief order.

Part 1 - Conditions which must be met

575.   This part of the schedule sets out conditions that the debtor must meet in order to obtain a DRO. The debtor must be domiciled in England and Wales on the application date or at any time during the period of three years ending with that date have been ordinarily resident or carried on business in England and Wales. He must not be an undischarged bankrupt, subject to an individual voluntary arrangement or a bankruptcy restrictions order. Neither must he be subject to a debt relief restrictions order or have had a debt relief order made within the 6 years prior to the determination date. If the debtor is subject to a bankruptcy petition that petition must be disposed of before a debt relief order can be made. The schedule imposes limits on the permitted level of overall indebtedness (the amount of which is prescribed in an order), a limit on the debtor's permitted surplus monthly income (also prescribed in an order) and a limit on the value of the debtor's property (also to be prescribed in an order).

Part 2 - Other conditions

576.   This part of the schedule sets out other conditions which the debtor must meet in order to obtain a DRO, specifically that he must not have entered into a transaction at an undervalue or given a preference to another person within the two years prior to the application date, and the determination date. This is in order to avoid a situation where the debtor has disposed of his assets in order to meet the permitted criteria for obtaining a debt relief order, and to protect the position of creditors.

Schedule 19: Schedule 4ZB to the Insolvency Act 1986

577.   Debtors who are guilty of misconduct that has in some way contributed to their insolvency will be subject to an enforcement regime that encompasses restrictions orders in the same way as bankruptcy. Schedule 19 sets out who may apply for a debt relief restrictions order or undertaking, possible grounds for obtaining one and gives details as to the timing of an application, the duration of the order or undertaking. Such orders may last from 2-15 years and will serve to protect the public from the culpable debtor. Whilst subject to a restrictions order, the debtor will remain subject the same disabilities as those imposed by the original order – for example he will not be able to obtain credit beyond the prescribed amount without disclosing his status.

Section 109: Debt management schemes

578.   This section defines "debt management scheme" as used in this Chapter.

579.   Subsections (2) to (4) set out conditions that must be met by all schemes that are seeking approval. Schemes must apply only to individual debtors (i.e. not companies or partnerships) who do not have any debts incurred in the course of business. Schemes may be open to all such individuals or to particular categories (as defined by the particular scheme). Schemes must also allow any debtor to whom the scheme applies to ask that a DRP be arranged. Where such a request is made, the scheme operator, (or an authorised person under the scheme), must decide whether a DRP is appropriate for the debtor (in accordance with the terms of the scheme, some of which may be prescribed under section 111), and if so, arrange the plan.

580.   Subsection (5) specifies that the operator of an approved scheme must be a body of persons, (for example, a company or a partnership rather than an individual).

Therefore it would be possible for a body such as Citizens Advice, or an existing repayment scheme provider such as the Consumer Credit Counselling Service or Payplan, or for a private company, to operate an approved scheme. But it would not be possible for an individual to do so.

Section 110: Debt repayment plans

581.   This section defines "debt repayment plan" as used in this Chapter. Subsections (2) to (4) outline conditions that must be satisfied by a plan.

582.   Subsection (2) introduces the concept of "qualifying debts" and provides that the plan must specify all of the debtors "qualifying debts". Section 132 provides that a "qualifying debt" is any debt, except for a debt that is secured against an asset, such as a mortgage, or which cannot, by virtue of the terms of the DMS (i.e. terms set by the scheme operator), be included in the plan. (Regulations under section 111 could have the effect of prescribing other classes of debt that may not be included by any scheme, by making such terms a condition of approval).

583.   Subsection (3) requires the plan to provide for full or partial payment of the debts specified in accordance with the plan.

584.   Subsection (4) makes it clear that it does not matter if a plan requires different amounts to be paid in respect of a specified debt at different times or the payments are insufficient to satisfy the debt in full. (Section 114 provides that in these circumstances the remainder of the debt would be written off provided that the debtor had complied with the terms of the plan).

Section 111: Approval by supervising authority

585.   This section enables a supervising authority (see section 129) to approve DMSs. It also permits the Lord Chancellor to make regulations prescribing both the conditions that must be satisfied for a scheme to be approved and any considerations that the authority must or must not take into account when considering a request for approval. These conditions and considerations may, in particular, relate to any of the matters listed in Schedule 21. These include the constitution, governance, size and financial standing of the scheme operator, and the terms and operation of the DMS. Regulations could, for example, specify minimum levels or periods of repayment.

Schedule 21 – Regulations under sections 111 and 113

586.   This Schedule specifies provisions that may be made in regulations as to conditions or considerations about the approval of a scheme under section 111, and as to the terms of approval of a DMS under section 113.

Section 112: Applications for approval

587.   This section allows the Lord Chancellor to make regulations specifying an application procedure for the approval of DMSs, and provides that such regulations may enable a fee to be charged for an approval application.

Section 113: Terms of approval

588.   This section provides that an approval will be subject to terms that may be specified in regulations or in the terms of the approval itself. Such terms might include the duration of the approval, (which could be given for a defined period, for example, for 5 years). Different types of schemes might be approved for different periods. On the expiry of an approval, a fresh approval could be sought. Such

regulations might also make provision as to termination of an approval other than by expiry, (for example, termination of an approval if terms of the approval are breached). Other terms to be specified in regulations could include particular requirements that may be imposed on the scheme operator covering such matters as the continued operation of the scheme, and the provision of reports relating to the operation of a scheme.

Section 114: Discharge from specified debts

589.   This section specifies that a debtor is discharged from the debts specified in the plan only when all of the payments required under the plan have been made. This allows debts to be partially written off, providing the terms of the plan have been complied with and all the necessary repayments made.

Section 115: Presentation of bankruptcy petition

590.   Sections 115 to 118 impose requirements on certain creditors during the currency of a DRP or during a period of protection. (Period of protection is defined at section 133). These sections are based on similar provisions for AOs and EROs (set out at Chapters 1 and 2 of Part 5 of the Act respectively).

591.   The first requirement, in section 115, provides that any qualifying creditor of the debtor (section 131 defines "qualifying creditor") is to be prohibited from presenting a bankruptcy petition against that debtor, during the currency of a DRP, unless regulations provide otherwise or he has the permission of a county court to do so. This section also defines the currency of the plan as beginning when the plan first has effect and ending when the plan ceases to have effect.

Section 116: Remedies other than bankruptcy

592.   This section sets out the second requirement. It prohibits, during a period of protection, qualifying creditors from seeking to recover their debt by pursuing any other remedy (that is, other than bankruptcy), unless regulations provide otherwise or the creditor has permission of a county court.

Section 117: Charging of interest etc.

593.   This section sets out the third requirement; during a period of protection, qualifying creditors are prohibited from charging any interest, fee or other charge in respect of a qualifying debt unless regulations provide otherwise or the creditor has permission of a county court.

Section 118: Stopping supplies of gas or electricity

594.   This section sets out the fourth requirement. In this case, during a period of protection, domestic utility creditors (as defined in subsection (2)) must not stop the supply of gas or electricity or the supply of any associated services unless one of the exemptions mentioned in subsections (4) to (7) applies.

Section 119: Existing county court proceedings to be stayed

595.   This section provides that any county court proceedings that were pending against the debtor when the DRP was arranged, must be stayed if the following conditions are met:

- the proceedings relate to a qualifying debt of the debtor's and they are not bankruptcy proceedings;

- the creditor under the debt is unable to enforce it because of the prohibition referred to in section 116 (remedies other than bankruptcy); and

- The county court, in the proceedings, which are to be stayed) has notice of the DRP.

596. Where proceedings are stayed under this section, the county court has discretion to allow the creditor any costs incurred in the stayed proceedings. A scheme operator may, if asked to do so by the debtor or creditor, add those costs to the amount specified in the plan in respect of that debt so long as the operator is not under a duty to terminate the plan (for example, because the new total debt exceeds the scheme's maximum).

Section 120: Registration of plans

597. This permits regulations to provide for the registration of either an application for a plan to be made or a plan coming into existence in the register of judgments, orders and fines, and enables section 98 of the Courts Act 2003 to be amended by such regulations for this purpose. Registration would provide a mechanism by which potential lenders could check whether a person had applied for a DRP or was currently subject to a DRP.

Section 121: Other debt management arrangements in force

598. This section defines the relationship between DRPs and the other debt management arrangements set out in subsection (7), which are AOs, EROs and DROs. It provides that when a DRP is arranged, it cannot come into effect unless any other debt management arrangement which had effect in relation to the same debtor immediately before the plan was arranged ceases to have effect.

599. Subsection (3) provides that any provision (whether in the plan or elsewhere) about when the plan is to come into effect is subject to the provisions of this section.

600. Provision is also made for the scheme operator to notify the provider of the other arrangements as soon as practicable, or as soon as it becomes aware of their existence, of the approval of the plan. Similar provisions are incorporated in the revised AO and ERO schemes and in the new DRO scheme. This will ensure that no more than one debt management arrangement has effect in respect of the same debtor at the same time.

Section 122: Right of appeal

601. This section introduces the term "affected creditor" which is defined as a creditor with a debt that has been included in the DRP.

602. Subsection (2) allows affected creditors to appeal to a county court against the fact that a plan has been arranged, that their debt has been included in the plan or the terms of the plan but subsection (3) makes it clear that affected creditors may not appeal against the inclusion, in a DRP, of a debt owed to another creditor.

Section 123: Dealing with appeals

603. This section applies if an appeal is made to a county court under section 122. It provides that the court may order the scheme operator to:

- reconsider the decision to arrange a plan;

- reconsider the terms of the plan;

- modify the plan; or

- revoke the plan.

604.   Additionally, this section allows the court to make interim provisions in respect of the period before the appeal is determined.

Section 124: Charges by operator of approved schemes

605.   This section allows the operator of an approved scheme to recover its costs from either debtors or affected creditors (defined in section 131(1)) or both. The definition of "costs" in subsection (2) will ensure that only reasonable costs are charged.

Section 125: Procedure for termination

606.   This section allows regulations to specify a procedure for terminating the approval of a scheme. This procedure may require the supervising authority to give notice and reasons, conditions that must be met and a period that must elapse before the termination takes effect.

Section 126: Terminating an approval

607.   This section provides that a scheme may only be terminated in accordance with the following:

- any terms which the approval is subject to under section 113;

- any provisions made in regulations under section 125; or

- any other provisions made under this Chapter.

Section 127: Alternatives to termination

608.   This section allows regulations to provide for alternatives to termination of an approval. Such regulations may provide for the transfer of the operation of a scheme to another body (to include transfer of the scheme from the scheme operator to the supervising authority itself). Such a transfer might be appropriate in order to protect debtors and creditors where, for example, the operator of the scheme no longer meets the terms of approval, but the scheme itself does comply with any relevant terms.

Section 128: Effects of end of approval

609.   Where the approval of a scheme comes to an end (for whatever reason), this section enables regulations to specify what effect this will have on existing DRPs under that scheme. The section provides an important safeguard for debtors by allowing such regulations to specify that plans can continue to operate, where appropriate, as though the scheme is still approved or as though the plan had been made under a different approved scheme.

Section 129: The supervising authority

610.   This section defines the "supervising authority" (the person who approves DMSs), and specifies that that the supervising authority can be either the Lord Chancellor or a person authorised by the Lord Chancellor. This section therefore enables the Lord Chancellor to delegate his approval powers (for example, such powers might be delegated to a judicial or existing national advice body).

Section 130: Regulations

611.   This section empowers the Lord Chancellor to make regulations under this Chapter. Regulations will be subject to the affirmative resolution parliamentary procedure on the first occasion they are made under any section or thereafter if regulations are made under section 118(6), if regulations under section 120 amend primary legislation or if regulations amend sections 122 or 123. Otherwise they will be subject to the negative procedure.

Section 131: Main definitions

612.   The section sets out the main definitions for this Chapter.

Section 132: Expressions relating to debts

613.   This section defines a "qualifying debt" as any debt that is not secured against an asset or which cannot, by virtue of the terms of the DMS, be included in the plan. A "business debt" is defined as a debt incurred in the course of a business.

Section 133: Periods of protection

614.   This section defines a "period of protection" as a period beginning when a debtor asks for a plan to be arranged and, if a plan is not arranged, ending when the decision not to arrange the plan is made. Where a plan is made, the period of protection ends when the plan ceases to have effect. The definition is however subject to subsection (4) which provides that where other debt management arrangements are in force immediately proceeding a debtor's request for a plan to be arranged, the period of protection does not begin until the plan is both arranged and comes into effect. This prevents debtors being simultaneously subject to different schemes.

PART 6: PROTECTION OF CULTURAL OBJECTS ON LOAN

SUMMARY

615.   Part 6 provides immunity from seizure to objects which have been lent to this country from overseas to be included in a temporary exhibition at a museum or gallery. Immunity will be given from any form of seizure ordered in civil or criminal proceedings, and from any seizure by law enforcement authorities. It will apply to objects of any description which are owned by a non–resident person or an institution and which are lent for temporary exhibitions to the public at any approved museum or gallery in the United Kingdom. The immunity will apply provided that the import of the object in question complies with the law on the import of goods, and that the museum or gallery has published information about the object as required in regulations made by the Secretary of State.

BACKGROUND

616.   Under the previous law, the United Kingdom has given immunity only to objects which are covered by the provisions of the State Immunity Act 1978. The absence of a more general immunity for works of art and other cultural objects which are lent to temporary exhibitions in this country has made museums and private owners in other countries increasingly reluctant to lend to such exhibitions without a guarantee that their art treasures will be returned. Provisions in Part 6 will enable such a guarantee to be given.

COMMENTARY ON SECTIONS: PART 6

Section 134: Protected objects

617.   Section 134 defines the conditions that need to be met for an object to be protected from seizure and specifies where and for how long the protection will be given.

618.   Subsection *(2)* provides that an object will only be protected if five conditions are satisfied: the object must usually be kept outside the United Kingdom; it must not be owned by anyone resident in the United Kingdom; the import of the object must comply with the law on the import of goods; it must be brought to the United Kingdom to be displayed to the public in a temporary exhibition at a museum or gallery and the museum has complied with regulations requiring publication of information about the object. The Secretary of State is given power to make such regulations.

619.   Subsection *(4)* provides for the extent of the protection. An object must only be in the United Kingdom for the permitted purposes (defined further in subsection (7)) and, with one exception, the protection will only last for twelve months. It is only intended to protect from seizure objects which are being lent for the purposes of a temporary exhibition. Objects on long term loans to museums will not be protected.

620.   Subsection *(5)* provides for the single exception to this rule. Where an object has been damaged since coming to the United Kingdom, and is being repaired, conserved or restored in this country, it will continue to be protected until it has left the United Kingdom following the completion of the repair, conservation or restoration.

621.   Subsection *(7)* ensures that objects will only be protected if they are on display in a temporary exhibition at museums, undergoing related repair, conservation or restoration, or travelling to or from the place where they are being displayed or repaired/restored. Subsection *(8)* defines the repairs, conservation or restoration which will be considered to be related for these purposes.

622.   Subsection *(9)* gives the Secretary of State a power to require a museum or gallery to provide further information about an object to inquirers. The information which must be produced, the circumstances in which it must be produced, and any conditions on the production of information may be specified in the regulations. This power is additional to the power given to the Secretary of State in subsection *(2)* to require museums and galleries to publish particular information about an object.

623.   Subsections *(10) and (11)* make further provision in relation to the regulations to be made under subsections *(2) and (9)*. The regulations may only be made with the consent of the devolved authorities, and they will be made by statutory instrument, subject to the negative resolution procedure.

Section 135: Effect of protection

624.   Section 135 defines the effect of the protection and sets out the limited circumstances under which it is not available.

625.   Subsection (1) ensures that where seizure or forfeiture of an object is required to enable the UK to comply with its obligations under EU or international law, the object concerned will not be protected. This could apply where, for example, the

court is asked to enforce an order for the seizure of an object made by the courts of another country to confiscate proceeds of crime.

626.   Subsection (2) ensures that the protection given to an object loaned to an exhibition does not give any protection from prosecution to those dealing with the object, where the dealing in question constitutes an offence.

627.   Subsection (3) clarifies the extent of the protection which will be given to objects under this Act. It includes immunity against all forms of execution which might be made against an object protected under the Act, any order made in civil proceedings and any measure taken in criminal proceedings (or for the purposes of a criminal investigation) which might affect the control or custody of an object. The protection given is intended to exclude any form of seizure or detention of an object lent to an exhibition in this country whether by a claimant to the object, a creditor or by law enforcement authorities.

Section 136: Relevant Museums and Galleries

628.   Section 136 defines "museum or gallery" for the purposes of Part 6. Only objects which are loaned to those institutions which have been approved by the relevant authority will qualify for immunity under this Part.

629.   Subsection *(2)* sets out the factors to which the approving authority must have regard in deciding whether or not a particular institution should be approved. These are the institution's procedures for establishing the provenance and ownership of objects, and whether it complies with guidance published by the Secretary of State on such procedures. This list is not exclusive. The approving authority may also take account of other factors in deciding whether an institution should be approved.

630.   Subsection *(3)* makes it clear that once approval has been given, it may be withdrawn, and identifies two situations in particular which are likely to lead to the loss of approved status. These are if an institution's procedures for establishing the provenance and ownership of objects are deemed to be inadequate, and if an institution fails to provide information on request as required in regulations. The approving authority may however also consider other factors.

631.   Subsection *(4)* clarifies the effect of withdrawal of approval. Those objects which are already in the museum or in the United Kingdom en route to the museum on the date on which approval is withdrawn will not lose their approved status. However, objects which are loaned to the museum after its approval has been withdrawn will not qualify for immunity.

632.   Subsection *(5)* identifies the appropriate authority. The Secretary of State will be responsible for approving museums and galleries in England. Each of the devolved administrations will be responsible for approving museums and galleries in their respective countries.

Section 137: Interpretation

633.   Section 137 contains interpretation provisions for Part 6.

634.   "Public display" is defined to include any display to which the public have admission, except displays with a view to sale. The immunity will not apply to any objects which are included in an exhibition organised by art and antiques dealers or auctioneers to advertise works for sale, or to publicise an auction.

635.   This section also sets out the rules for determining whether an individual, the trustees of a settlement, a partnership or a body corporate should be considered to be resident in the United Kingdom.

Section 138: Crown application

636.   This section provides for Part 6 to apply to the Crown, and agents of the Crown, in the same way as to all other persons and institutions.

PART 7: MISCELLANEOUS

SUMMARY

637.   Part 7 enables High Court enforcement officers to execute writs of possession issued to enforce compulsory purchase orders, and removes the obligation for enforcement of such writs from High Sheriffs. This Part also amends subsection 31(5) of the SCA 1981, reproducing and extending the effect of the existing judicial review provision. In particular, it provides that where the decision maker in question is a court or tribunal and the decision is quashed on the ground that there has been an error in law, the High Court will be able to substitute its own decision where, without that error, it is satisfied that there would have been only one decision which the court or tribunal could have reached. Part 7 also changes the way in which ACAS negotiated settlements are enforced and reforms the process for hearing design right appeals.

BACKGROUND

Compulsory purchase

638.   Currently, there is an anomaly as regards the execution of High Court writs in that High Court enforcement officers and High Sheriffs are able to execute High Court writs of execution, but only High Sheriffs are able to enforce writs of possession issued to enforce compulsory purchase orders. The proposed changes will align the enforcement of compulsory purchase orders with the regime for enforcing High Court writs of execution contained in section 99 of and Schedule 7 to the Courts Act 2003.

Enforcement of ACAS brokered agreements

639.   The Advisory, Conciliation and Arbitration Service (ACAS) has no enforcement powers of its own. *Transforming Public Services* undertook to simplify the system so that an award of compensation, whether ordered by an employment tribunal or agreed between the parties (under compromises involving ACAS), can be enforced with the minimum of bureaucracy as if it were an order of the civil courts. The Act makes such agreements enforceable in England and Wales as if they were sums payable under a county court order, and in Scotland by diligence as if the certificate were an extract registered decree arbitral bearing a warrant of execution issued by the sheriff court.

Appeal in relation to design rights

640.   The Registered Designs Appeal Tribunal (RDAT) was created by section 28 of the Registered Designs Act 1949. Any appeal from the registrar (the Comptroller-General of Patents, Designs and Trade Marks) under that Act lies to the RDAT. The Act transfers the jurisdiction of the RDAT to the Patents County Court and the High

Court in England and Wales, the Court of Session in Scotland and the High Court in Northern Ireland.

COMMENTARY ON SECTIONS: PART 7

Section 139: Enforcement by enforcement officers

641.　　This section amends the Lands Clauses Consolidation Act 1845 and the Compulsory Purchase Act 1965 to enable writs of possession issued to enforce compulsory purchase orders to be executed by High Court enforcement officers.

642.　　This change aligns the enforcement of compulsory purchase orders with the regime for enforcing High Court writs of execution contained in section 99 of and Schedule 7 to the Courts Act 2003. It does not remove the right of a sheriff to enforce a writ of possession issued to enforce a compulsory purchase order, should one be directed to him and should he wish to enforce it. The section removes the obligation, with the attendant legal responsibilities and liabilities, to enforce such writs of possession (High Sheriffs being unpaid volunteers who are appointed annually).

Section 140: Supplementary and Schedule 22: Compulsory purchase: consequential amendments

643.　　Section 140 amends Schedule 7 to the Courts Act 2003 to enable the arrangements that are currently in place for enforcement officers executing High Court writs of execution, (identifying enforcement districts, providing for administrative arrangements for enforcement of such writs and extending to enforcement officers powers and obligations that sheriffs have under common law), to be extended to High Court enforcement officers executing writs of possession issued to enforce compulsory purchase orders.

644.　　Schedule 22 makes consequential amendments in connection with the above.

Section 141: Judicial review: power to substitute decisions

645.　　This section replaces the existing section 31(5) of the SCA 1981 and extends the power of the High Court in respect of quashing orders. The High Court will still have the power to return a matter to a decision maker with a direction that it reach a decision in accordance with its findings. However, where the decision maker is a court or tribunal and the decision is quashed on the ground that there has been an error of law, the court will, alternatively, be able to substitute its own decision for that decision if it is satisfied that without the error there would have been only one decision that the court or tribunal could have reached.

646.　　Unless the High Court directs otherwise, a substitute decision will have effect as if it were a decision of the relevant court or tribunal.

Section 142: Recovery of sums payable under compromises involving ACAS

647.　　Section 142 amends the Employment Tribunals Act 1996 to provide that sums payable under ACAS negotiated settlements are enforceable in England and Wales as if they were sums payable under a county court order, and in Scotland by diligence as if the certificate were an extract registered decree arbitral bearing a warrant for execution issued by the sheriff court. In each case, the sum is not recoverable if the person by whom it is payable obtains a declaration in the relevant jurisdiction that the sum would not be recoverable from him under the general law of contract.

648.		Rules of court may make provision as to time limits within which an application to a county court (or, in Scotland, a sheriff) for a declaration that a compromise sum is not recoverable is to be made; and when an application (whether made to a county court, the sheriff or an employment tribunal) for a declaration that a sum is not recoverable is pending.

Section 143: Appeals in relation to design rights

649.		Section 143 abolishes the Registered Designs Appeals Tribunal and diverts its jurisdiction in England and Wales to the Patents County Court and the High Court concurrently. The Patents County Court is one with which users are familiar, is experienced in design matters, and its rules allow for affordable representation by patent agents and efficient procedures. While the Patents County Court and the High Court have concurrent jurisdiction, it is intended that appeals must first come to the Patents County Court which can then decide whether the appeal should be transferred to the High Court. The RDAT's Scottish jurisdiction is transferred to the Court of Session and its jurisdiction in relation to Northern Ireland to the High Court in Northern Ireland. The courts to which cases from the Isle of Man are to be diverted can be prescribed by an Order in Council under section 47 of the Registered Designs Act 1949.

650.		The RDAT also has the power to deal with some appeals on (unregistered) design rights pursuant to section 249 of the Copyright, Designs and Patents Act 1988. Design rights are rather different in nature to registered designs and are more complex, as they raise issues that are much more akin to copyright than registered designs. Section 143(3) therefore provides that in England and Wales and Northern Ireland, appeals relating to design rights are to be heard by the High Court and that, in Scotland, appeals will lie to the Court of Session.

PART 8: GENERAL

SUMMARY

651.		Part 8 provides for the territorial extent of the provisions of the Act. It also provides for provisions of the Act to come into force in accordance with orders made by the Lord Chancellor (or by the Secretary of State in relation to Chapter 3 of Part 5 or the Secretary of State or the Scottish Ministers in relation to Part 6), and confers power on the Lord Chancellor (or on the Secretary of State in relation to Chapter 3 of Part 5) to make transitional and consequential provision by order.

COMMENTARY ON SECTIONS: PART 8

Section 144: Protected functions of the Lord Chancellor

652.		Section 144 makes all the Lord Chancellor's functions under (or under amendments made by) Part 1, sections 51 and 57, Parts 3 and 4, Chapters 1 and 2 of Part 5 and certain functions under, or under amendments made by, Part 2 protected functions for the purposes of section 19(5) of the CRA 2005, so that they cannot be transferred to another Minister without primary legislation.

Section 145: Power to make supplementary or other provision

653.		Subsection (1) allows the Lord Chancellor (or the Secretary of State in relation to Chapter 3 of Part 5) to make an order for supplementary, consequential and transitional provisions, while subsection (2) makes it clear that such an order can amend or repeal other enactments. This type of provision is not unusual in Acts which reform existing statutory schemes and therefore require transitional provisions and/or which have a large number of consequential amendments, see for example the Courts Act 2003.

Section 146: Repeals

654.   Section 146 introduces Schedule 23. Schedule 23 lists repeals arising from, among other things, the new statutory framework for tribunals and the new, unified law on enforcement.

Section 147: Extent

655.   By virtue of section 147, Parts 1, 2, 6 and 8 of the Act extend to England and Wales, Scotland and Northern Ireland and Parts 3, 4, 5, and 7 extend only to England and Wales. This is subject to subsections (4) and (5). Subsection (4) allows for amendments to other Acts to extend to the same extent as those other Acts. For example, the amendment made by section 142 will extend to Scotland (as well as to England and Wales). Subsection (5) extends certain provisions to the Isle of Man. This is because section 143(1) and (2) amends the Registered Designs Act 1949, which itself extends to the Isle of Man. Therefore section 143(1) and (2), the relevant provisions of the repeals Schedule and section 147 extend to the United Kingdom and the Isle of Man.

Section 148: Commencement

656.   Section 148 provides for the Lord Chancellor (or the Secretary of State in relation to Chapter 3 of Part 5 or the Secretary of State or the Scottish Ministers in relation to Part 6) to specify commencement dates for provisions in the Act by order. The provisions in the Act other than sections 53 (Transfer from salaried to fee-paid judicial office), 55 (Appointment of deputy Circuit judges), 56 (Appointment of deputy district judges, etc.), 57 (Deputy, and temporary additional, Masters etc.), 60 (Appointment as Chairman of Law Commission), 145 (Power to make supplementary or other provision), 147 (Extent), 148 (Commencement), 149 (Short title) or Schedule 11 (District judges and deputy district judges) will come into force on days appointed by order. Sections 53, 55, 56 and 57 and Schedule 11 come into force on Royal Assent. Sections 145 and 147-149, as is usual for general provisions of this sort, also come into force on Royal Assent; and section 60 comes into force two months after Royal Assent.

GLOSSARY OF ABBREVIATIONS

ACAS   Advisory, Conciliation and Arbitration Service

AIT   Asylum and Immigration Tribunal

AJTC   Administrative Justice and Tribunals Council

AO   Administration Order

AEA 1971   Attachment of Earnings Act 1971

AEO   Attachment of Earnings Order

CCA 1984   County Courts Act 1984

COA   Charging Orders Act 1979

CLSA 1990   Courts and Legal Services Act 1990

CPR 1998   Civil Procedure Rules

CRA 2005   Constitutional Reform Act 2005

CRAR   Commercial Rent Arrears Recovery

DAC   Discipline and Appeals Committee

DMS   Debt Management Scheme

DRO   Debt Relief Order

DRP   Debt Repayment Plan

DTI   Department for Trade and Industry

DWP   Department for Work and Pensions

ERO   Enforcement Restriction Order

HMRC   Her Majesty's Revenue and Customs

IVA   Individual Voluntary Arrangement

JAC   Judicial Appointments Commission

MoJ   Ministry of Justice

RDAT   Registered Designs Appeals Tribunal

SCA 1981   Supreme Court Act 1981

HANSARD REFERENCES

Stage	Date	Hansard reference
House of Lords		
Introduction	16 November 2006	Vol. 687 Col. 100
Second Reading	29 November 2006	Vol. 687 Cols. 759-805
Committee	13 December 2006 and 14 December 2006	Vol. 687 Cols. GC43–GC80 and GC81–GC138
Report	31 January 2007	Vol. 689 Cols. 238-306
Third Reading	20 February 2007	Vol. 689 Cols. 1007-1024
Lords Consideration of Commons Amendments	17 July 2007	Vol. 694 Cols. 154-157
House of Commons		
Introduction	21 February 2007	N/A

Second Reading	5 March 2007	Vol.457 Cols. 1296-1362
Committee	15 March 2007 20 March 2007 22 March 2007 24 March 2007	Public Bill Committee on Tribunals, Courts and Enforcement Bill 1st Sitting Cols. 4-28 2nd Sitting Cols 32-68 3rd Sitting Cols. 73-106 4th Sitting Cols. 110-148 5th Sitting Cols. 152-172 6th Sitting Cols. 176-212 7th Sitting Cols. 216-248
Report and Third Reading	27 June 2007	Vol. 462 Cols. 340-438

Royal Assent - 19 July 2007

House of Lords Hansard
Vol. 694 Col 363
House of Commons
Hansard Vol. 463 Col 429

Printed in the UK by The Stationery Office Limited
under the authority and superintendence of Carol Tullo, Controller of
Her Majesty's Stationery Office and Queen's Printer of Acts of Parliament

8/2007   377656   19585